D0663789

Cat Companions

ALSO BY SUSAN M. SEIDMAN

The Pet Surplus:
What Every Dog and Cat Owner
Can Do to Help Reduce It

CAT
COMPANIONS

*A Memoir of
Loving and Learning*

SUSAN M. SEIDMAN

Contents

Cat Companions

· 1 ·

Special Relationship

The late humorist Will Rogers is popularly quoted as having said "I never met a man I didn't like." Those weren't his exact words, but they aptly convey how he felt about people. I can say much the same for the way I feel about cats.

True, over the years I've met the occasional cat I didn't care for. Perhaps it had an unnaturally foul disposition, or an untypically homely face. (A smashed-in Persian puss always puts me off.) But most felines never fail to appeal. My usual response was succinctly described by a man who took me to dinner one night in Paris many years ago:

We were walking away from the restaurant along a cobbled street in the Latin Quarter. Suddenly I stopped in my tracks, peering down a side alley at something I'd seen moving. Pointing to it with a beatific smile, I turned to my friend. "Don't tell me," he said. "You have that dotty expression on your face. You must have just seen a cat."

Millions of us like cats. You surely do or you wouldn't have opened this book. But my guess is that only a minority of us are dotty enough about them for a relationship in a class by itself — incontestably more special than with other members of the animal kingdom. (Be reassured! You needn't belong to this fanatic coterie to appreciate the book.)

Why do people like me feel this way? It's irrational, of course. We can expound endlessly on the beauty, grace, charm, dignity, subtlety, playfulness, cleverness and resilience of felines, on their gifts for empathy and love and tranquil companionship.... All these qualities, while emphatically true, aren't convincing *reasons* for doting on cats as we do. Our intimacy and interdependence with them rest on emotion and resist explanation.

But this special relationship doesn't exclude a love of animals in general. Most "cat people" I know are also very fond of dogs and horses and birds and other household pets. They care about the well-being of farm animals and wildlife. They join and support local and national humane organizations. I do have the impression, though, that dedicated "dog people" are not only far more numerous, but feel nowhere near as warmly toward cats as cat people feel toward dogs. (Am I being unfair?) I myself happen to love dogs — albeit not as promiscuously and uncritically as I love cats. There are times I regret my long-standing decision, for reasons I'll soon explain, to forego canine companionship in my own home.

Also, for a good part of my adult life — nearly a quarter-century — I deliberately chose to forego the company of cats. *That* decision stemmed from an eye-opening lesson in our pets' emotional dependence on our presence — as vital as their physical dependence on our care. (Details in the chapter on Supan.)

So my cat-keeping history is erratic. One feline pet in my childhood; another in early adulthood. Then a long fallow period, relieved only by a few part-time boarders: friends' cats parked with me temporarily while their owners traveled out of town. Finally, the day came when I felt ready for a lasting, wholehearted commitment to full-time pets of my own. That happened in early 1975, coinciding with a couple of watershed changes in my life. Ever since then, my home has always been enhanced by at least two cat companions. And I heartily hope it always will be.

Here, I've brought together the stories of 21 cats who have lived with me throughout my life — all but two within the past three decades. Even though three of these pets stayed only very briefly, for one good reason or another, they're included because I learned something of value from each experience. A few others remained for several months or more, but again had to move out early. The rest — a dozen cats in all — settled in as permanent, fully integrated members of my family to the end of their lives. (With one glaring exception: Tim.)

Why publish a chronicle of my cat companions?

Partly to indulge myself — in fond reminiscence. To me, each pet is memorable. Each life story is worth revisiting. Flipping through the pages of my cat notebooks, poring over the snapshots, I can once again celebrate their unique qualities and recall the pleasures of their company.

Partly, too, I want to share with others who keep cats — whether they're prompted by casual friendship or (like me) incurable addiction — the wealth of joys, sorrows, smiles, trials, comforts, chores and surprises that living with these fascinating creatures has afforded me. Some lighthearted moments will invite readers to smile in recognition. Some stressful episodes could shock or disturb. Other anecdotes should enlighten and entertain.

Most of all, I want to pass along a number of useful lessons I've learned. Years of hands-on experience with so many different cats have taught me volumes about the nature, needs, behavior, care and quirks of their inimitable species. (One example: I've discovered how widely the bonds of affection and dependence can vary in our relations with individual felines — *and* in the relations between felines sharing a home.) Ideally, fellow catkeepers will find at least a few new insights and practical tips to benefit their own households.

Before proceeding with cats, let me pay brief but affectionate tribute to the other inimitable pet species. I said I'm very fond of dogs, but I've shared a home with only two in my lifetime. Rusty, a spunky little Irish terrier, was my first childhood pet — until he chased one car too many on our suburban street. (Hours later, hemorrhaging from internal wounds, he dragged himself upstairs to die where he always faithfully slept: under my father's bed.) As I recall, my mother was too upset by the experience to ever consider acquiring another dog.

The other dog who lived with me did so only temporarily, for a few short stays. He belonged to a good friend whose work periodically took her out of town. During each business trip her pet, a handsome ruddy and white collie-shepherd mix named Sammy, moved into my city apartment. He was a dear, gentle, companionable, beautifully behaved guest. I grew so attached to him that I didn't even resent the obligatory early-morning walks, every day in every kind of weather. Normally I consider such rise-and-shine outings an insufferable chore — by far the biggest deterrent to urban dog ownership.

There were also a couple of summers when Sammy's mom and I shared a rented beach cottage. I loved watching him race happily along the sand, cavort gleefully in the surf, reveling in the freedom and fresh air of his country weekends. Once, in a quiet bay, he and I even enjoyed a swim together side by side. It was a wonderful portrait of the good life for a deserving dog. I made a mental note to provide it for a dog of my own some day — *if* I ever moved full-time from the city to the country.

But when I eventually did make that move, some ten years later, I had second thoughts. It looked as if my responsibilities caring for a dog, even in the carefree countryside, might weigh too heavily against my rewards from his companionship.

Safety was a key concern. I couldn't just open the door every morning and let my dog run loose around the neighborhood; there were far too many cars speeding along my street. (I could never forget what happened to poor Rusty.) My yard didn't easily lend itself to being completely fenced in. And never in a million years would I dream of confining a dog outdoors on a chain. So some kind of secure enclosure would have to be specially built and maintained for my pet's exercise and sanitation needs. Or, alternatively, I'd have to take him on leashed walks three or more times a day — exactly as if we lived in a city.

Here, my own sloth kicked in as a factor. To put it mildly, I'm not a morning person. The prospect of sticking to a mandatory schedule of outings each and every day of my dog's life — not to mention arranging substitute care every time I planned to be away from the house more than a few hours — put a serious damper on my enthusiasm.

Call me selfish; you'd be right. But advantages should outweigh disadvantages in our lifestyle decisions, don't you agree? When we commit ourselves to the responsibility of keeping a pet (or raising a child, for that matter), we *must* anticipate that the gains will be greater than any inconveniences. As I foresaw it, the special benefits promised by a dog's companionship — romps together on the beach, strolls in the woods, excursions in the car, other shared outings that rarely (if ever!) appeal to cats — didn't quite compensate for the special chores involved in a dog's day-to-day care.

Another factor: As noted, I'm choosy about dogs. My attraction to them is far more discriminating than my unbridled passion for cats. Of course I could easily become attached — deeply — to a wonderful pet like Sammy. I wept when I learned of his death, though I hadn't seen him for some time. Every now and then, while out and about, I see a dog I find captivating enough to want to kidnap on the spot. (More often than not it has a foxy face and a silky coat; for sheer looks, shelties and Siberian huskies are my favorites.) Normally, though, I judge each canine objectively on its particular merits. And some — because of appearance or behavior or both — don't appeal to me that much. This is emphatically *not* the way I judge cats.

My decision to forego a dog was clinched by one final consideration. By the time the right moment arrived, after I had moved full-time to the country, my home was already populated with cats. Two had been in residence for a couple of years and a third soon joined the household. Strictly in terms of space, I could certainly have fitted in a medium-size dog. (The minimum size I'd consider!

If you want a little pet, I always say, then get a cat.) But there would have been, at the least, a tricky adjustment phase — maybe a trial-and-error period of choosing the right cat-compatible dog — to meet all the animals' competing needs for psychological "space," attention from me, coexistence with each other.

So it ultimately made most sense for me, the one resident human, to limit my pets to one species. I could then best concentrate on their well-being and my bonding with each.

Next question: how many pets? This pretty much took care of itself, as key decisions in my life usually have. My preferred solution has been to keep a minimum of two cats, a maximum of four, at any given time.

Why not just one cat — at least for starters? Because of one early, unsettling experience with a solitary pet. (You'll find details in the chapter on Supan.) It convinced me to never again subject an animal to such a lonely existence whenever I'm absent from home. Perhaps I'm a bit neurotic on this point. If an "only" cat has a dog around for company, of course that makes for a different situation. I've also known single-cat households with no other animals — though with at least two human companions — where the pet *seems* contented enough. And once I even had an extraordinary cat who, of his own free will, moved out on me and his three fellow felines, opting instead for a life as Only Pet in a neighbor's home. (Details in the chapter on Tim.) Even so, as a matter of hard-learned principle, I won't risk worrying ever again about a miserably lonesome little creature, longing for my return home every moment I can't be there.

A second cat is certainly no guarantee against feeling bored and bereft if their owners have to be away for long stretches. The two pets may not be particularly enamored of each other. They can't keep themselves busy and entertained playing Scrabble or pingpong or debating the state of the world. A TV set tuned to *Animal Planet* or a video of fluttering birds can hold their attention for just so long. Indeed, they're likely to spend most of their time asleep — even if a radio is left on playing soft music for them. But each one remains aware of another living presence in the home. At the least, this should lessen any sense of isolation while their people are absent and raise the comfort level for both animals.

Purely as a practical matter, two cats can be accommodated as comfortably, and nearly as cheaply, as one. Even the tiniest studio apartment or trailer has room for a pair of felines to claim their personal space, chase each other for exercise, clamber up and down a scratching post, cavort with a jingling ball or catnip mouse. One litter box, one water bowl, one double-well feeding dish suffice to serve both. Food for a second cat, even premium brands, adds only cents a day to the budget.

Veterinary care is a more substantial expense. But once the all-important spay-neuter surgery has been paid for, then regular annual checkups and booster shots normally remain affordable for many years. By the time complications of advancing age raise the animal's medical bills (just like our own), most of us are far too devoted to our longtime pet to resent the additional cost.

I've long been convinced that a "starter set" of two is the way to launch a cat family. When I worked as a volunteer adoption counselor at a local humane society, I used to urge cat seekers who had no other felines at that point to look for an appealing *pair* to take home together. Double adoption doesn't just help to speed more orphaned animals out of shelters into homes. For an adopting family, it has the huge advantage of forestalling acceptance problems between their new animals.

By nature, every cat has a powerful instinct to establish and defend its personal territory. The longer an "only" resident cat rules the roost, the harder its adjustment to a newcomer is likely to be. *But* when two pets simultaneously start a new life together in brand-new surroundings, neither one has time to stake out proprietary turf. So they naturally accept each other's presence as part of the unfamiliar new setting that both must adapt to.

That doesn't necessarily mean that the two will form a close attachment — though of course we always hope they will. The easiest and most affectionate pairings are usually two kittens from the same litter, or a kitten with its mother. But there's no reason two unrelated cats can't live happily together as siblings in their new adoptive home. If they're no longer little kittens, however, it's a good idea to introduce them first, and observe their initial reactions to each other, *before* taking them away from the shelter. I had occasion to do this once with a couple of year-old females. Their names were Lucy and Rosalie — my own initial starter set. Their relationship, as you'll see, worked out beautifully.

After that dual adoption, all subsequent members of my cat family were introduced one at a time. A few were additions, expanding the nuclear family to three or four cats. But most were filling a vacancy left by a departed cat.

Note that I avoid the word "replacement"! Whether a pet has died or moved elsewhere, whether the attachment between us was close or casual, I consider each one unique — thus irreplaceable. In physical looks alone, each of my random-bred cats has been distinctive enough not to resemble any predecessor or successor very closely. The one exception, many years ago, was my seal-point Siamese, Supan. Naturally, I thought she looked identical to all other seal-point Siamese — but I never acquired another one to confuse me!

Here, a snide sidebar: I don't really understand purebred-dog fanciers who persist in "replacing" each beloved golden retriever, poodle, dachshund, Jack Russell, black Lab, or whatever they've buried, with a virtual clone of the departed. Do they find individual personality traits to appreciate in each new specimen of their favorite breed, bestowing qualities distinct from the late pet it visually duplicates? Or do they just group the whole series of "replacement" dogs together in their minds as a single generic pet? The same questions, of course, could be asked of pedigreed-cat fanciers — but there are many fewer of these.

Back to numbers. Why did I settle on a maximum of four cats at any one time? For both logistical and emotional reasons.

As the sole full-time occupant of a small house, I can comfortably accommodate the indoor needs of three or four pets — equipment, toys, room to play and private places to snooze — without crowding or competition for personal space. It helps, too, that my cats can spend time outdoors in pleasant daytime weather. They have freedom to roam and explore. The fresh-air exercise and variety of things to see and do — and hunt! — helps keep them fit, alert and entertained. It also lightens my own caregiving chores. My litter boxes need changing and my scratching posts need replacing much less often than if they were used by indoor-only cats. (As for the safety risks of an indoor-outdoor lifestyle, already mentioned in connection with dogs, I'll deal with this in detail later.)

But the practical advantages of a small cat family are less important to me than the amount of individual attention and affection it allows us to share. I cherish a one-to-one relationship with each of my pets. I want to be able to concentrate on every cat's particular needs and count on enjoying quality time together, just the two of us.

A couple of people I know have successfully managed multi-cat households of anywhere up to a dozen — or more — pets. These are *not* to be confused with pathological "collectors" (also called "hoarders") of animals, whose negligent and slovenly operations we usually learn of after they've been raided by the animal-control police. On the contrary, my softhearted acquaintances have taken conscientious care of their multiple pets in a clean and wholesome environment. They are Good Samaritans whose rescue impulses got a bit out of hand. They simply couldn't refuse to take in — or turn over to a shelter — any appealing stray who needed help. So their menageries just grew, spontaneously, like Topsy.

While I respect their dedication, I'd never choose to follow their example. In my time I've rescued several neighborhood strays. But with a couple of exceptions, to be related, I had no wish to add these orphans to my own household. The only "extra" cats I've felt equipped to cope with, only occasionally and temporarily, were foster kittens — no more than two at a time. A pair of littermates could spend a few weeks in my guest room, cozily segregated from the resident pets, until the shelter I volunteered with was able to place them in permanent homes.

Over the years, I've found the preferred size for my cat family to be three. (As it is at this writing.) A third pet adds the spice of variety and a challenge to complacency. It helps keep an established cat couple — that "starter set" — from getting bored with each other's company. Once, a hardship case swelled my population to four. That lasted seven years. Afterwards, however, I wasn't tempted to square the triangle again. On a couple of occasions, after losing one member of a long-resident trio to illness, I waited many months before trying to fill the vacancy. The two survivors (no longer young) and I myself all needed ample time to grieve and adjust to the absence of our cherished companion.

You and other readers won't all agree on the optimum size of a cat family — or a good many other choices I've made. What I'm setting down here are just subjective views from my personal experience. I'd never expect my preferences to work for every other catkeeper the way they have for me. In this book you'll find no rigid rules, no tablets handed down from the mountain, no gospel preached by much-quoted "experts." In fact, some of my opinions — such as on letting cats circulate freely outdoors — defy the prevailing wisdom among most veterinarians and animal-care professionals.

Still, I hope you'll find some nuggets of useful knowledge, a few fresh insights, and more than a few valuable tips. My efforts will be rewarded if the book helps to enrich your relationship with your own cat companions. That relationship is, after all, special — agreed?

A half-century ago one of the great cat writers of all time, Paul Gallico (also an acclaimed sports writer, journalist and novelist), created a small masterpiece. He called it *The Silent Miaow — A Manual for Kittens, Strays, and Homeless Cats* (Crown Publishers, 1964). The book, illustrated by photographer Suzanne Szasz, was purportedly "translated from the feline" by Gallico from a manuscript discovered on his neighbor's doorstep. In it, the "author" instructs her fellow cats, step by step, how to select a desirable home, move in, win over the hearts of family members — and gradually take total control of the household.

Her conquest techniques will be instantly recognizable to anyone who has ever been Taken Over by a pet feline. If *The Silent Miaow* isn't hopelessly out of print, I hope you can locate a copy to enjoy. Meanwhile, here are stories about some of the cats who captivated and took control of me.

· 2 ·

Tiger

First Experiences

Rusty, the hapless Irish terrier, was our first family pet. Tiger, who joined the household a few years after Rusty's death, was our first and only cat. He arrived during the early phase of World War II, when I was 12 or 13. Tiny Tiger, recently weaned, must have been between eight and ten weeks old.

The remarkable thing is that he was allowed into the house at all.

My mother strongly disliked cats. I think she was afraid of them. You've probably known people like her: visibly nervous in the presence of a cat, cringing if the animal comes near enough to pose the threat of an ankle rub or a jump into the lap. (And they, of course, are just the people cats find irresistible and unfailingly make a beeline for.) Who can explain this visceral dread? Certainly it's incomprehensible to cat fanciers — though I'm sure many of us harbor similar repugnance to some other forms of animal life. I myself have little use for creepy-crawlies like caterpillars and large hairy insects. However, as my mother later demonstrated, an aversion *can* be subdued, if not wholly overcome.

Her laundress' cat had produced a litter and my mother was urged to take the last remaining kitten. She knew I'd be delighted. Apparently my special attraction to cats was already apparent from my reaction to those we saw around the neighborhood. So, gamely but gingerly, she brought the squirming little tabby home in her empty laundry bag.

Later, from the vantage of adulthood, I realized that my new pet kitten represented more than just a brave effort by my mother to surmount her antipathy to cats. In retrospect it was the most generous gift she ever gave me — indeed, her *only* wholly unselfish gesture of love toward me that I can, or choose to, remember. You'll infer, correctly, that she was a self-centered human being and that we were never close. (To pursue this theme would involve quite a different book — one that I don't want to write and you wouldn't care to read.)

Though Tiger was nominally "my" pet, I had little responsibility for his care. His food was dispensed with a sneer by Ada, our big, gruff, surly housekeeper who heartily loathed "That

Cat." (During wartime, cheerful and cooperative domestic help was a luxury beyond the means of families like ours.) Of course I would have loved to have Tiger snuggle up to sleep with me every night — but this was a no-no. A cat, like a dog, was forbidden upon any of the furniture. My mother was deeply enamored of her house and furnishings, maintained in pristine condition. She was also abysmally ignorant of a house cat's intrinsic nature and needs. Indeed, we all were — including my easygoing father, who grew quite fond of Tiger but always treated him like a small dog.

To ensure that our furry new family member wouldn't shed all over her upholstery while the household slept, my mother decreed that Tiger must spend nights in the cellar. (I don't recall that she ever tried to provide him with a special pet bed. If so, he declined to use it, as cats usually do.) Our basement wasn't uncomfortable; on chilly nights he could curl up near the furnace on soft towels or a scatter rug. But it was pretty lonely. Before Ada arrived in the morning and let him upstairs to be fed, he could if he wished get out into our yard through a small flap my father cut into the basement's outer door.

The main purpose of his exit flap, naturally, was for answering calls of nature. We had nothing resembling a litter box. Clay kitty litter, in fact, didn't even appear on the market until after World War II. Up to then, owners of indoor-only cats used sand, garden soil or shredded newspaper to fill a toilet tray. But in our suburban community virtually all pet cats led indoor-outdoor lives. So Tiger, just like a dog, was expected to be housebroken enough to do all his business outside, in all weather fair or foul.

Indeed, he never soiled inside the house. But on nasty nights, why leave his cozy dry basement for the discomfort of the cold and rain outside? Instead, he chose to relieve himself in the coal bin. This was no longer in active use; our family had switched to an oil furnace early in the war. So the coal pile from past deliveries just sat there — very inviting to a latrine-digging cat. We always knew when Tiger had availed himself of this facility; the next day his white mitten paws were heavily smudged with soot until he took the time for a good wash. But my parents didn't really object. They never went near the coal bin (whose aroma grew increasingly fetid throughout Tiger's years with us) and apparently considered the alternative — providing *and maintaining* a sanitary box for him — even more unpalatable.

I discovered something else about cats' sanitary habits. One day I spotted Tiger sitting upright in a flower bed, immobile, apparently lost in deep contemplation. He looked so fetching that I impulsively went over to pick him up for a hug. But he resisted my embrace. I soon discovered why, as a cascade of urine dribbled over my clothes. Lesson! From that day forward I knew enough never to disturb a cat sitting absolutely still on garden soil in profound concentration.

But there was another, unforgettable occasion when Tiger refused to budge from his spot in the garden. This time he was lying down — and gravely ill. For several days he had hardly moved or eaten. He felt very hot to the touch. Frantic with worry, I insisted on taking him to the vet as soon as possible. My mother grudgingly interrupted her supper to drive us there, while I cradled poor feverish Tiger in my lap, wrapped in a towel. (Another unheard-of item in those days was a carrier designed for small pets.) The doctor's verdict was grim: pneumonia. Tiger was admitted to the hospital and spent quite some time there; I don't remember whether it totaled days or weeks.

Luckily my pet survived, thanks to two things. The new "miracle drugs" penicillin and sulfanilamide had recently become available for veterinary as well as human use. (My father, in fact, would surely have died of lobar pneumonia in the same period without the benefit of then-novel antibiotics that we take for granted today.) Tiger's other great piece of luck was his exceptionally dedicated and compassionate veterinarian, Dr. Vine.

In my youth, every family that cared about its pets "had" a vet, but the pets spent a lot less time there. Regular exams and vaccinations were the exception, not the rule; moreover, few vaccines had been developed by then. Spaying and neutering house pets was rare without some compelling medical reason. Basically, you took your dog or cat to the doctor when it fell sick, or was hurt in an accident, or had some problem related to breeding or giving birth. Before our dog Rusty had his last, fatal encounter with a car, his fractured bones from chasing earlier vehicles had been mended on at least two occasions.

We turned to Dr. Vine when Rusty's old vet had retired. He was young and very up-to-date on the newest techniques and research to help his small patients. I was thrilled, of course, when he succeeded in saving Tiger from the deadly pneumonia infection. But in retrospect, the very best thing he did for my pet — and for my own education in petkeeping — was a different matter entirely.

Tiger was free to roam the neighborhood by day or night. Weather permitting, he exposed himself to all kinds of nocturnal delights and dangers. They *must* have included amorous encounters with receptive females — as well as territorial brawls with other tomcats on the prowl. He began coming home with bloody wounds from some of these fights. After a few hospital visits to stitch his lacerations and medicate his abscesses, Dr. Vine suggested that we have him neutered.

I was horrified, protesting — with all the wisdom of my 14

years — that his manhood was as precious as life itself. Dr. Vine prevailed by reminding us, first, that Tiger had already enjoyed a good couple of years sowing his wild oats, and second, that as he got older he was bound to lose more battles, suffer more crippling injuries, even get himself killed. So we consented to his castration. After that, he never fought again and settled down to life as a placid, somewhat plumper stay-at-home cat.

Macho or eunuch, Tiger was always affectionate. He and I bonded from the start. A day or two after he first arrived, I decided to introduce him to the neighborhood by taking him on a nice, long walk (just like my dog!). As I strode along the fields and unpaved paths, I looked back from time to time to check that my new pet was keeping pace. There he was, a tiny bundle of fur not yet three months old, plodding doggedly behind me to keep from being abandoned. The poor little creature must have been exhausted; I finally picked him up to carry the rest of the way home. With time, of course, I learned that a cat's exercise requirements are vastly different from a dog's. Our most companionable moments were spent quietly cuddling and snoozing together.

My father's quality time with our pet focused on bedtime food treats. When my parents came home from an evening out, more often than not Tiger heard their car drive up and was waiting for them on the stoop. Otherwise my father would whistle from the back door. Soon, the little bell on Tiger's collar would jingle in response as he cantered up to join us in the kitchen. Next, my father would take some salami or other delectable cold cut out of the fridge. He'd slice enough for his own snack, then chop up extra little pieces to drop on the floor, one by one, for his ecstatically appreciative "customer." He was basically a dog man, who enjoyed pampering Tiger as if he were a midget canine.

Our pet's major impact, though, was on my mother. She had,

as I said, a longstanding aversion to cats. Whatever event in her past may have provoked this, she never told us. But Tiger managed to soothe her anxiety and overcome her repugnance. He came into her life as a helpless and adorable little kitten — and she loved babies of all kinds. As he grew, she in turn grew accustomed to his feline ways and warmed to his loving personality. Indeed, in the only surviving photo I have of Tiger, she is holding him tenderly on her lap.

Inevitably, my mother became generally more comfortable around cats. I won't exaggerate by claiming that a single pet transformed her from cat hater to cat lover. She was always nervous in the presence of strange adult felines, feeling threatened by any sudden, unpredictable change in their behavior. But in later years she didn't flinch from approaching, even handling, my own feline pets. Once she even adopted a new kitten of her own, whom she named Janine. Alas, Janine — obtained from the litter of some local merchant's cat, and obviously never seen or vaccinated by a veterinarian — soon succumbed to a virulent bout of distemper. My mother, devastated, never tried again.

Tiger himself contracted a grave kidney infection while I was away at boarding school. Although Dr. Vine did his best, as always, our pet couldn't survive. I wept when my parents wrote me the news but took comfort knowing that Tiger had lived a pretty nice life — albeit not a very long one — with our family.

Farewell, my first cat! A full decade would go by before I acquired my second.

Supan

A Lasting Lesson in Companionship

Every pet seems to qualify as a "first" or an "only," one way or another. Supan fit both categories. She was the first pet I owned as an adult, fully responsible for supporting myself and my animals. She was also my only purebred cat (to date, at least). Even so, while I paid for her food and equipment, I didn't need to provide her daily hands-on care. And though I had paid to purchase her, the price was token. The seller wasn't a professional breeder, simply a family seeking homes for their own pet's new kittens.

She lived with me barely more than a year. Yet she taught me a profound and enduring lesson in what the term "companion animal" means.

Here's the setting: Time, early 1950's. Place, Paris. I, fresh out of college, had moved there to start my adult life working at the American Embassy for the Marshall Plan economic aid program. After a year or so I ran into a former school friend from England who worked at the British Embassy, and we took a furnished apartment together on the Rue des Belles-Feuilles in Passy. It came fully equipped with a live-in housekeeper, Berthe. She was a warm and motherly soul, committed to the meticulous care of her French employers' flat (the owners were then living abroad), and a splendid cook. Luckily for me, she was fond of animals and agreed to help look after the kitten I wanted to bring home.

The Siamese had been advertised in a house newsletter circulated among Embassy staff. When I went to collect her, I found myself in an elegant mansion occupied by the family of an attaché named Douglas MacArthur — no, not the famous general but a younger relative of his. As I recall, they charged me 5,000 francs (then worth about $15) for my new kitten, showing me her mother's pedigree papers.

I chose to call her Supan — hoping it was authentically Siamese — after seeing a photo of a glamorous Thai movie star by that name in *Life* magazine. She fit instantly and happily into our household. On weekdays, while my roommate and I were away at work in our respective embassies, Supan and Berthe enjoyed each other's company at home. Evenings and weekends, when we dined in on Berthe's delectable menus and held open house for friends on Sunday afternoons, my little pet was spoiled with attention. Berthe grew to dote on *"ma petite fille,"* with only a rare grumble about having to keep the litter box cleaned.

Although we lived a few stories up, Supan had access to fresh air through French windows opening onto a balcony. One day, after a confrontation outside with the concierge's roving cat, she came back with a small but conspicuous nick in her ear. (Much like the notch deliberately cut nowadays by rescuers of feral cats in trap-neuter-release programs, to identify the animals that have already had spay-neuter surgery.) It occurred to me then, and many times since, that this might be one of the the few ways to tell one purebred pet apart from others of the identical type.

I once attended a Parisian cat show in which a group of Jean Cocteau's favorite cats — every one Siamese — were on display. Could he really distinguish one from the other? I asked his pets' caregiver. She assured me that indeed he could. Yet I wondered: If I walked into a room filled with seal-point Siamese the same age and weight as Supan, would I be able to pick out my own cat? Or would she have to recognize and find me? I suppose the same dilemma holds true of any purebred without an individual pattern of markings — like, say, a black Lab or a white Persian.

Supan's, and my, idyllic life in Berthe's attentive care didn't last very long. Our landlords were returning home from overseas to reoccupy their Paris apartment. My roommate and I, while remaining good friends, decided to move into our own separate new quarters. With Supan, I settled into another pleasant apartment in Passy, on the Rue Lalo. It belonged to a French military family I knew, then stationed in one of the country's West African colonies.

Though the flat also came with a maid (I don't recall her name), the situation was very different. Her wages, instead of being covered by the agreed rent as Berthe's had, needed to be paid out of pocket each month that I wanted to keep her. She didn't live upstairs in the same building, as Berthe had. Instead, she left for home right after fixing my early, solitary supper on nights I didn't eat out. (Here, I couldn't really entertain guests.) I was basically employing her just to clean the flat, shop for my food and — above all — look after Supan's needs and keep her company during my weekdays at the office.

A costly cat sitter! But Supan sorely needed company. Not only was she sociable and demonstrative by nature. She'd now become accustomed to having people around and thrived on attention. When I came home after the long workday, sometimes extended by an outing to dinner or a movie with friends, my little cat was almost desperately eager to see me. She snuggled close to me every night, under the bedcovers when cold air blew through the opened window — which reminds me of a comic-opera adventure we shared.

One chilly November evening I shampooed and set my hair. When I emerged from the bathroom, Supan was nowhere to be found. She'd escaped out through the partly open French door to our small balcony. Then she had jumped a few feet down and across to a neighboring rooftop. There she found herself trapped, pacing back and forth and complaining loudly. I, shivering in my bathrobe with my wet hair in curlers, hung over the balcony railing beseeching her to jump across into my welcoming arms. But she was frightened by the short open space that she had to leap over and up to get back to her home. Nor could I see any way for me to get across to her roof to rescue her. What to do?

At last, inspiration: we needed a bridge! Any firm plank a few feet long would do. I fetched my landlady's ironing board. It stretched perfectly over the gap between the edge of Supan's roof and my waiting arms atop the balcony rail. She took a few minutes to test how solid the footing was, stepping gingerly on and off, whimpering, while I murmured nonstop encouragement and endearments. (The scene was worthy of a Marx brothers movie. I've always regretted the absence of a witness with a camera to record it for posterity.) Finally, Supan mastered her fear and raced up the plank to my embrace.

Her other outdoor adventure was planned — and a lot pleasanter. One mellow fall weekend I had a visit from the fiancé of one of my college friends. He was passing through town and wanted to see how typical Parisians spent their Sunday afternoons. So, with Supan in tow, we went for a stroll in the Bois de Boulogne. She had a small collar and leash. But it wasn't easy to "walk" her and she spent most of the outing perched on my shoulder. Many admiring ooh's and ah's from passing pedestrians, especially children. Supan was, of course, a striking beauty — and not the typical pet one sees in a public park.

An interesting postscript to that day: Stan, my visitor, told me much later that it was the first time in his life — he was then in his late 20's — that he became aware of an allergy to cats. Just the few hours he spent in Supan's presence brought on respiratory symptoms he had never noticed before. They worsened in subsequent years every time he went near a cat. (Indeed, it's not at all rare for adults to begin suffering allergic reactions that never bothered them as children. And vice-versa. In my late teens, for example, I outgrew a sensitivity to certain foods that used to provoke acute attacks of eczema in my childhood.) To this day Stan — who has always refused to dose himself with antihistamines or immunization shots — can't ever spend an evening in a home where a cat lives, or even where a cat *has* lived recently. He and his wife, my longtime friend, live several hundred miles away. Over the years I've visited their home a number of times and she, by herself, has come to stay with me. As long as I keep cats, he can never accompany her.

A few months after Supan and I moved to the Rue Lalo I became eligible for home leave, having worked at the Embassy for two years. This meant an extended vacation in the United States, plus two-way transatlantic travel time (always by ship in those days), all at State Department expense. Arrangements for the maid during my projected six-week absence were simple: I let her go. But what to do with Supan?

I was relieved to find a lucky solution through my office. Michèle, a French girl who worked in my division, adored cats; so did her parents and sister. The family already had one of their own, a neutered male Persian, and offered to take Supan into their apartment the entire time I planned to be away. I was happy to deliver her to Michèle's welcoming home, leaving a financial contribution for her food and my own family's American address in case any problem arose.

At the outset, Supan and the incumbent Persian hid under separate pieces of furniture hissing strenuously at each other — the standard reaction, of course, when a strange cat intrudes on a resident's established territory. But the two felines had begun sniffing and getting used to each other even before I left Paris a few days later. Eventually they became best buddies. Reassured that my pet was in responsible hands, I took off on my vacation.

As for what I might do about her lonely life on the Rue Lalo after my return — I left that dilemma till later.

Midway through my home leave, an urgent letter from Michèle's mother arrived. Supan, it seems, had been in heat almost constantly since my departure. She was miserably uncomfortable, squirming and yowling from the pressure of her raging hormones. She also put on a shameless public performance, rubbing, rolling and displaying in front of the young men who came calling on Michèle and her sister — an embarrassment for the entire, very proper French family.

Madame wrote that she had taken Supan to see their veterinarian. He diagnosed an ovarian cyst, and advised that the only way to cure her estrous condition was to spay her. (This was expensive major surgery. In Europe, as here, it was still quite uncommon in an era *before* pet overpopulation induced many families to have their female pets routinely "fixed.") Did I authorize them to go ahead and have Supan operated on immediately? Or did I prefer to wait, and decide what to do after I got back to Paris?

Of course I gave my permission by return mail. I apologized for the trouble my poor, overheated little cat had caused and promised to cover all expenses.

When I arrived back in France, Supan was still at the animal hospital convalescing from her ovariohysterectomy. I visited her there with Michèle's mother, caressing her as best I could with the thick surgical dressing wrapped around her midsection. Meanwhile, I told Madame, I'd been giving serious thought to Supan's future. Much as I doted on her, I realized it was self-indulgent of me to subject my pet to those long hours at home alone, just for the sake of our short times together nights and weekends. Indeed, I had become reluctant to accept social engagements outside of home, knowing how fervently Supan needed, waited for and thrived on my presence there.

So, I explained, I was prepared to sacrifice the love and pleasure of keeping Supan — *if* she could be securely resettled in a good home like Madame's. There, surrounded by a family of four, she'd have the company of one or more people most of each day — plus a fellow cat to play with. What did Madame think of the idea? Would they be interested?

Her face broke into a smile of relief. They had all become so attached to Supan, she confessed, that they weren't looking forward one bit to seeing her leave. Indeed, they'd be delighted to have her come live with them permanently.

And so she did — at least as a permanent member of their family. A couple of years later Michèle got married, to a rare-book dealer who shared her love of cats. So the newlyweds took Supan along with them, to the book-lined apartment on the Left Bank where she would live happily ever after. The last time I saw her was a day they invited me over for lunch. Supan was comfortably ensconced on a radiator cover. When I tried to kiss her she bit me on the nose. I can't say I blamed her.

After my repatriation to America a few years later, I lost touch with Michèle and her husband except for the occasional Christmas card. Today, the only photo I have of Supan is a closeup shot they sent me of an elegant, mature sealpoint, looking serene and cherished.

I've never once regretted my "abandonment" of her to a far more sociable — thus more suitable — home environment.

And I've never wavered in my conviction, learned the hard way from the experience with her, that *no* pet should be kept to spend just a few brief hours together that happen to fit into a busy owner's daily schedule. It's not just unforgivably selfish of the owner; it's cruelly unfair to the animal. If a dog or cat lover doesn't have enough free time for sustained, regular companionship with his pet — especially when it's the *only* pet in the home — then it would be kinder and wiser to forego the relationship entirely. At least, postpone it until such time as the owner's lifestyle permits more frequent togetherness with his companion animal.

After Supan, that's just what I myself did — for the next 22 years.

· 4 ·

The Long Intermission
A Few Guests and A False Start

From the parting with Supan in early 1953 until the start of 1975, I led a petless life — by deliberate choice. Of course my affection for cats never flagged. Of course it was a sacrifice to deprive myself of a nurturing feline presence. But I was able to justify my stubborn solitude with two rationalizations. One, compassionate, was reluctance to subject any new pet to the long hours of loneliness Supan had endured.

My other motive was unabashedly selfish. I cherished my freedom too much. I was determined not to feel tied down by practical *or* emotional commitments to a creature wholly dependent on my care. I was enjoying the busy life of a young career woman in New York — having settled there in autumn 1957. I liked being free to go out with friends any evening, go out of town on weekends, travel far and wide on vacation…in short, go where I pleased when I pleased with *no* obligations at home to worry about.

Still it was nice, on occasion, to have some soft cuddly company at home — with no long-term engagements. (If this sounds suspiciously like the marriage-shy bachelor who'll commit to nothing beyond his one-night stands — well, I guess the shoe fits.) I let it be known among friends and colleagues that friendly four-footed guests were welcome for short stays in my apartment when their owners had to be away.

Over the years I had several "boarders." (No money ever changed hands, though a couple of owners insisted on supplying their pets' preferred food.) My first feline visitors were Pearl and Prince Hal, a mother-and-son combo. Both had bright orange coats; she was a shorthaired tabby and he was a drop-dead-gorgeous longhair. I had in fact suggested his name when he was a kitten; his flaming red-gold hair recalled paintings of England's young king Henry VIII. The cats belonged to the couple on eastern Long Island from whom I rented a weekend cottage for eight consecutive summers. They were off to a midwinter vacation in the Caribbean and happy to offer their country cats a brief taste of high-rise life in the city. I don't recall much about their stay but have a nice snapshot of the pair relaxing on my bed, taken by a professional photographer friend. I did make the useful discovery that a single litter box — all that would fit in my tiny urban bathroom — comfortably serves the full-time needs of two housebound cats.

Next, a brown tabby who belonged to a friend of a friend moved in for about a week. I don't remember her name; only that she was "well-behaved and very affectionate," as promised by her owner, and slept on my bed every night.

After that came two cats belonging to Kay, another freelance photographer I knew. She had to leave town on assignment from time to time — once going as far as Brazil. I've forgotten her cats' names but remember them vividly from their two visits.

Kay's male pet was a longhaired mixed-breed, entirely black. The female was a skinny blue-point Siamese. Both were well into middle age and were served special diets that I had to follow to the letter. Their stays with me were pleasant and uneventful — up until the last evening of their second visit.

Suddenly, I heard ear-shattering shrieks from the Siamese in the next room. I ran in. She was just sitting on the floor yelling her heart out. What was wrong? What should I do? I could see no injuries, and wondered if something she'd eaten might have provoked a severe gastric pain. Or — and this was too dreadful to contemplate — had she swallowed something sharp, like a needle dropped on the rug from my sewing box, and was now in the throes of a fatal internal hemorrhage?

I was frantic with worry. Should I rush the poor creature off to an emergency veterinary clinic? First, I decided I'd see if Kay had returned from her trip — she was due back that very night. Luckily she had just come home and answered the phone. I described the scary symptoms. Kay reassured me; it only meant that her cat was in heat.

What!! This nine-year-old house pet had never been spayed? Kay had had the black tomcat neutered years ago (otherwise he would have been impossible to live with in a city apartment). But she'd chosen to keep the pedigreed Siamese intact, perhaps with some notion of eventually breeding her to a suitable stud. Now, she insisted, the animal was too old to risk spay surgery. Kay coped with the noise and stress of her heat cycles by giving her tranquilizer pills. Did I have any handy? No, I never used them, but I did have ear plugs. And that's what I relied on to get some sleep, until Kay could get there next day to pick up her pets.

Kay was a bit of a flake. She was devoted to her cats but had made a truly dumb decision not to sterilize both of them at the outset. Now, the senior Siamese was condemned to endure the discomforts of estrus several times a year for the rest of her life (unless mercifully freed by feline menopause, if that exists). Here was a cautionary lesson I had been spared only because my own unspayed Siamese, Supan, had developed a reproductive complication while still young. But I'd take that lesson to heart from now on: *every* cat should be fixed, early!

My hospitality during the petless years wasn't wholly restricted to cats. As mentioned earlier, I entertained a lovely large dog, Sammy, on two or three extended visits.

Our three walks every day, plus extended outings on weekend afternoons, introduced me to a hitherto unfamiliar world of dog people, dog etiquette and dog interaction. In one small enclosed park in my neighborhood, dogs were able to run off-leash, despite official prohibitions, and it was a joy to watch Sammy cavorting freely with his fellows. Only once did I have to restrain him, warned by the owner of another large male dog that a dominance fight seemed to be brewing. Naturally, few males had been neutered.

Another memorable moment was a midnight walk on a crystalline New Year's Eve with Sammy and a human guest who was also spending the holiday with me. Fresh snow carpeted the quiet streets. As we strolled past one luxurious apartment building, with an impeccable doorman and a glowing Christmas tree visible in the lobby, Sammy chose his moment to pause, squat, and deposit a holiday tribute on the curb just opposite the entrance.

My friend and I laughed, waved a greeting to the doorman, and applauded Sammy's excellent taste in selecting a men's room.

I always missed Sammy's genial company after he returned to his own home — though I saw him often when I was invited there. And I missed the soft, purring presence of each departed feline guest. But what I didn't miss, frankly, were the obligations of caring full-time for a pet. What counted most of all was my freedom — from responsibility.

Once, my avoidance of commitment was put to an excruciating test.

A few days before my birthday in 1971, on a weekday evening, I was invited to an informal dinner with a half-dozen friends. The hostess said nothing about a party occasion. But lo! a birthday cake appeared for dessert. Then, with coffee, I was handed an elaborate greeting card signed by everyone present. Folded inside was a gift certificate from a shop called Fabulous Felines. It entitled me to choose any of their pedigreed kittens up to a value of X dollars. I forget the exact maximum but it was in three figures; pretty extravagant at the time.

I was thunderstruck. A major social crisis! I looked round the circle at the expectant, warmly smiling faces of my friends. They knew how much I loved cats; they were proud of their inspired gift idea; they all awaited my ecstatic thanks for their thoughtfulness. What they didn't know, alas — and what I could hardly spell out for them then and there — was that *I wasn't emotionally ready* to take on a pet of my own. (Actually, the ringleader who had organized the group gift knew me well and should have figured this out on her own. Why else would I have chosen to deprive myself for so long?) The prospect of actually having to accept their gift filled me with dismay. Another powerful deterrent was the idea of welcoming into my home a "designer" pet deliberately bred to be sold — while so many thousands of homeless cats and kittens were waiting in animal shelters to be adopted.

What to do? For the moment, obviously, I had to do the gracious, hypocritical thing. I thanked everyone profusely and promised to let them know as soon as I'd made my choice of a Fabulous Feline.

The next step was harder. In fact there were *two* acts remaining in the mini-drama of the unwanted gift kitten. First I had to persuade the management of Fabulous Felines why I'd rather donate the value of their gift certificate to a humane society, instead of using it to take one of their pedigreed pets. After that, I had to justify my decision to my friends.

I put on a pretty dramatic performance at the shop. My friends meant well, I insisted to the owner — a corpulent man with a pasty complexion. But, I explained, they didn't realize that I was emotionally ill-equipped at this stage of my life to assume round-the-clock responsibility for the well-being of a pet, even a pet as irresistible as each of his Fabulous Felines looked to be. (Most, incidentally, were Persian — then, as now, the most marketable product of breeders' kitten mills.) Finally convinced that I was too neurotic to entrust one of his little treasures to, he agreed to redeem the gift certificate for cash. I suggested he send a donation in the shop's name (thereby benefiting from a tax deduction) to the American Society for the Prevention of Cruelty to Animals, the city's largest shelter. But he preferred to refund the money directly and let me make my own contribution.

When I mailed my check to the ASPCA, I told them how honored I was that six friends were celebrating my birthday with a joint gift to such a worthwhile cause. Then, I had to write the same thing to my friends — and convince them how genuinely grateful I was *without* bruising any feelings. (If you picked out what seemed like the perfect gift for someone, would you appreciate learning that your recipient immediately gave it away to, say, a charitable thrift shop?) This called for delicate diplomacy, especially with the person who had conceived the idea and gone to the trouble of arranging matters with Fabulous Felines. I labored long over my letter. Apparently it did the trick. None of my friends ever mentioned the matter again — but not one stopped speaking to me.

So, conscience clear, I continued my free-of-commitment lifestyle. But this lasted only another three and a half years.

EVEN THOUGH THIS book is about my relationships with cats, I must digress briefly to talk just about myself. Bear with me; it's relevant!

In early summer 1974, I underwent a sudden, fundamental change in my outlook. Call it an epiphany, a watershed, a midlife upheaval (I'd reached my mid-forties) ... whatever the label, it brought a major shift in my attitude and priorities. I'll never fully grasp *why* it occurred. But I can easily pinpoint the event that triggered it: I quit smoking.

For about a quarter-century, since my junior year in college, I had smoked. My habit grew into a two-pack-a-day addiction, but I didn't mind being a slave to it and couldn't imagine even trying to stop. At worst, when I had a really bad cold and bronchitis cough, I'd attempt to alleviate the congestion by cutting *down* on my smoking. I remember my allotment system: one cigarette per hour, with an extra allowed at each mealtime. This added up to a maximum 20 a day, about half my normal consumption. It certainly helped me breathe a bit better until the cold ran its course. But I can remember checking my watch impatiently — wasn't it time yet for my 3 o'clock cigarette? — as the need for a nicotine fix grew more urgent each minute.

So it went until April 1974. Then I came down with a vicious respiratory infection, picked up on an overseas trip, that left me still helplessly coughing and unable to breathe deeply long after the sneezy phase had run its course. I consulted a new doctor, who promptly sent me for tests to a pulmonary specialist. The verdict: chronic bronchitis and early emphysema. (Nowadays, both ailments together with asthma are commonly lumped under the heading "chronic obstructive pulmonary disease," or C.O.P.D.)

The news was a shocker but not that much of a surprise. My father had been an asthma-emphysema sufferer for decades — and his own mother had died of a lung ailment just before I was born. Although he had by then lasted to his mid-70's, his condition was pretty wretched. And now I learned that the family scourge had been visited on me.

As my doctor explained that day, there is no treatment or cure for emphysema (as there can be for lung cancer). The best one can hope for is to *slow* the deterioration of the lung tissue. And the only thing I could actually *do* to encourage this is — you guessed it! — give up smoking. The doctor, himself a nonsmoker, sympathized with an addict's difficulty trying to quit. He offered me a tranquilizer prescription, if I felt this would ease the transition, or suggested I might want to join one of several group cessation programs — the smokers' version of Alcholics Anonymous.

I vividly recall coming out of his office and standing, stunned, in the brilliant spring sunshine on Park Avenue. I'd just been hit with what amounted to a life sentence — total abstinence from cigarettes. If I wanted to postpone my death sentence, I'd have to serve the time. How in the world could I manage this? After two and a half decades, would I be able to adapt to a smoke-free life? I firmly doubted it.

Here, the story can be condensed. Figuring to give myself the best chance, I enrolled in a program called SmokEnders. It was fairly new, heavily advertised, and highly endorsed by several people I knew. Instead of quitting cold turkey, the smokers gradually weaned themselves from cigarettes over a five-week period. They then followed up with a few more weeks of AA-style reinforcement meetings. I joined up with the best possible attitude. I was powerfully motivated by the awful example of my father's condition (this was five years before he finally died, at 80) and honestly determined to succeed in making this sea change in my life. But I honestly didn't believe I could do it.

It worked, though! I faithfully followed the SmokEnder script, skipping only the occasional item I found too silly to bother with (such as reciting "You're worth it!" to the bathroom mirror every morning). To my astonishment, the adjustment wasn't nearly as hard as I'd feared. Once the nicotine drained out of my system, deprived of the oral gratification of sucking in tobacco smoke hundreds of times a day, I stepped up consumption of compensatory pleasures: good food, good drink — and plenty of sugarless chewing gum.

Physically, I found a dramatic improvement. My smoker's cough vanished and I breathed much more easily. Food tasted better. Of course I gained weight. But I deliberately waited a few months, until I was fully used to the nonsmoking habit, before dieting to take off the surplus pounds. Why be a masochist and deny oneself everything at once?

Another, wholly unexpected benefit was a much lower threshold between sleep and wakefulness. Apparently nicotine had an upper-downer effect on me (though it doesn't on most of the other smokers I've compared notes with). Every night, throughout the years I smoked, I needed a lot of time to fall asleep after my last bedtime cigarette. The next morning, no matter how long I'd rested, it invariably took a while to emerge from groggy somnolence into clear alertness. I'd assumed it was the caffeine in my first cup of breakfast coffee that jolted me awake. But in fact it had been my first cigarette of the day *with* the coffee that did the trick! Without the cigarettes, I soon reverted to my long-ago childhood pattern of falling sound asleep and fully waking up quickly and easily.

What, you may ask, does all this have to do with keeping cats?

I'm getting there! The *psychological* rewards of my liberation from nicotine were at least as great as the physical benefits. Let's not belabor the details. Let's say only that I suddenly found myself feeling much happier about life in general — and much readier for new commitments in particular.

I can't really explain *why* my outlook changed so dramatically. But I'll never forget *when* this happened. It was early July. My nine-week SmokEnder program was coming to an end. Our group's final meeting was a farewell cocktail party, held in a cozy Italian bistro. I chose to walk there from my office after work. En route, I noticed a crowd of people in front of the skyscraper that housed the Columbia Broadcasting System. They were very quiet. Two police cars had pulled up. I peered around the spectators. There, on the esplanade, a couple of maintenance workers were picking up the shattered pieces of a woman. Presumably she had thrown herself to the pavement from on high. I glimpsed a mass of curly reddish hair as her head was placed in a sack. A few hand cameras clicked; hardly anyone spoke. Dazed, I continued on toward my SmokEnder party.

That Friday I went out to the country as usual. But this time, unlike most summer beach weekends, I wanted no guests or company. I felt a pressing need to be by myself, undistracted, to think things over. For two days I strolled and sunned and swam on my own and digested my new situation.

Here I was in my mid-forties, alive and free and still in pretty good shape. I'd just successfully kicked away a crutch — a quarter-century addiction that threatened my survival. And I'd just witnessed the hideous end of a woman (perhaps close to my own age, who knows?) who had chosen to self-destruct rather than deal with her own demons, whatever they may have been. Restless, I mulled over the Big Question: *Just how am I going to benefit from the new lease on life I've just bought myself?*

Miraculously, by the close of that weekend I had some answers — and had already begun to act on them.

My epiphany message could be summed up in a cluster of clichés: Enjoy! Go for it! Commit! Smell the roses! Nothing to fear but fear itself! The emotional effect was a sudden readiness to recognize whatever would give me most pleasure in life — and pursue it without inhibition. This new attitude, positive to the point of euphoria, buoyed my existence immeasurably for a long time. In practical terms it translated into three major steps:

That Sunday, even before returning to the city, I contacted a couple of real-estate agents about finding me a house to buy. Thanks to a recent modest windfall from a family business, I could afford the down payment on a home of my own in the community where I'd been a seasonal renter for a dozen years. And now, all of a sudden, the prospect of taking full responsibility for managing my own property no longer deterred me.

A second immediate step: consulting the Sunday paper's classified ads for job listings. I'd been getting a little bored with my work in recent months, but hesitated to seek a change. The timing, I felt, would be unfair to a longtime boss who had treated me well and deserved my loyalty. But now, again, I suddenly saw no reason to deprive myself of a chance to explore other opportunities. If a really tempting new job turned up, I'd somehow find a way to arrange a graceful departure from the old one.

In both cases, feeling *free* to act on my newly acknowledged desires gave me the quickest and greatest satisfaction. Eventually I did acquire my own house — though the closing took place a full year after that watershed weekend. And, failing to find an irresistible alternative job, I ended up staying on where I was. Finally my boss retired. His replacement turned out to be impossible to work with, so then I quit without hesitation.

The third step, translating my new outlook on life into action, came last. The following winter, soon after Christmas, it abruptly dawned on me that I very much wanted to have cats living with me. Not guests, not boarders, but full-time pets of my very own. At long last I was ready for commitment!

Emotionally, I felt confident that the rewards from cat companionship would easily outweigh any inconveniences of cat care. Logistically, the situation was far easier than years ago in Paris with Supan. Now I lived near my office and walked to and from work in minutes. Many days I could conveniently come back to the apartment for lunch; evenings, I was home more often than out. My travel was infrequent, and there would always be time to arrange for pet sitters before a trip.

Best of all, I'd never worry again about a single, lonely little pet waiting, oh so pathetically, for my return. I'd get not just one cat — but a starter set of two. They'd always have each other for company no matter how long I was kept away from home.

So, heart bursting with anticipatory love and excitement, I set out one February day in 1975 to find my new felines. Instead of the ASPCA, where I had donated the price of my unwanted pedigreed birthday kitten, I decided I'd look first for my pets at a smaller shelter closer to my home.

The outcome was disastrous.

The Bide-a-Wee Home Association is a privately funded, widely respected humane society in existence since 1903. They showed me into a large kennel room with both dog and cat cages. (Already a bad sign; nowadays few shelters house the two species together.) Since it was midwinter there were no small kittens, which I wasn't seeking anyway. But none of the adult cats had alert, outgoing personalities. Perhaps they were too intimidated by the dogs' noisy barking — which made it hard for prospective adopters to get acquainted.

Kiowa (solid black) and Janis (gray tabby) were sharing a cage — as they had shared a home before their owner relinquished them to the shelter. The two females were "maybe four to six years old" (the staff was vague) and had been there "a while" (equally vague). Even though they appeared apathetic to the point of lethargy, I felt sorry enough for them to take a chance. Pets of their mature age, I thought, weren't likely to appeal to many adopters. And as a pair, they did have the advantage of being fully accustomed to each other's company. Their clean bill of health was guaranteed by Bide-a-Wee.

What did I expect when I got them home? Perhaps an hour or two of exploring and adjusting to the new surroundings, as all my temporary boarders over the years had done. Instead, both cats immediately vanished from sight. In the following days I occasionally glimpsed Janis, cowering in the bathtub or warily approaching her food dish as I left the kitchen. Kiowa remained invisible, emerging to eat, drink and use the litter box only in the dead of night or when I was out. Eventually I discovered that her hiding place was behind the stove.

What had traumatized them to this extreme? Was it the unspecified "while" they had spent cooped up in the shelter amid the cacophony of barking dogs? Was it having being abruptly uprooted from a longtime home and family and consigned to life in a steel cage? Or had they both always been neurotic by nature — perhaps the reason why their family discarded them?

Whatever the cause, I felt helpless to effect a cure. What I sought was a mutually fulfilling relationship, not the role of caretaker to animals with emotional disorders. My gut feeling, after four days with no sign of improvement, was that I'd made a mistake in judgment that time was unlikely to rectify. On a snowy Lincoln's Birthday — not yet combined with Washington's in a single Presidents' holiday, so my office had the day off — I packed up both unhappy creatures for return to the shelter. Poor frantic Kiowa battled with all her might, screaming and clawing in terror, to resist being thrust into the carrier. By this point I was pretty traumatized myself. On our silent bus ride through the white blur of the nearly empty streets, the cats at last quieted down. But my own heart kept pounding, as much from a punishing sense of failure as from the stress of that farewell fight.

When I stomped in out of the snow to deliver Kiowa and Janis back to the Bide-a-Wee staff, I was regretful but not apologetic. The cats, I told them, had been given a good second chance in my quiet and comfortable home. Since they couldn't adapt to this welcoming new environment, it seemed doubtful they would do better elsewhere. Unless their original owners were willing to take them back, I suggested, the staff might want to acknowledge that they were unadoptable and have them mercifully put to sleep.

This was not, of course, what the "no kill" shelter's personnel wanted to hear. Their phone call to the cats' previous owners elicited the assertion that there had been "nothing wrong" with them at the time of surrender. (Almost certainly a self-serving lie, as I've learned from subsequent experience as a shelter volunteer.) Kiowa and Janis were bundled off back to their prison cage. Let's hope that, if not reclaimed by their original family, they were eventually put out of their misery. And I found myself blacklisted as a prospective adopter, denied the option of looking for any other pets at Bide-a-Wee.

With hindsight, I did two things right in this whole affair. I waited until I felt fully ready to make pets a permanent part of my life. And I sought out animals that genuinely *needed* a home from a source that rescues, cares for and rehabilitates unwanted pets.

But I also did two things wrong. I selected my new pets more on the basis of pity than compatibility. I was doing them a favor (and the humane society too, by taking two hard-to-place cats off their hands). But by disregarding other candidates that might have appealed to me more, I was doing no favor to myself. This sounds selfish. Yet it's been proved time and again — including my own subsequent adoptions — that a pet-owner relationship has the best chance of success when its benefits are *reciprocal.*

My other mistake, looking back, was impatience. My excuse, for what it's worth, is that I hadn't had enough experience at that point to know better. I may have gambled unwisely when I picked Kiowa and Janis in the first place. But then, instead of carting them back to the shelter after a mere four disappointing days, I should have allowed a week or two, at least, for them to get used to their new surroundings. They'd been through a bewildering ordeal and deserved a fairer period of adjustment. The end result might have been the same — a failed adoption — but I should have been less hasty in arriving at it.

My false start had been a bruising episode. Like the rider who falls off the horse, I didn't dare nurse my wounds too long before trying again. A colleague at work scoffed at my naiveté (what I'd felt was compassion) in taking on the burden of two maladjusted middle-aged animals. Instead, he urged me to go pick a nice, lively, lovable *young* pet (or two) from a big city shelter with plenty of eager cats and kittens to choose from.

That meant my next destination could only be the ASPCA. Ten days after Kiowa and Janis' stormy departure, I set out for this renowned facility, America's oldest humane society. And there, indeed, a happy ending awaited: I found the love of my life.

5

Lucy

My Little Love

Those are the words on her gravestone. Lucy was *sui generis.* No other pet, no matter how cherished, ever laid serious claim to her unique status in my affections. (Many years later, however, there *was* a runner-up you'll hear about.) She was my first pick of all the cats who have enhanced my home and life, continuously, for over three decades now.

All told, Lucy and I spent six years, seven months and 19 days together. Our relationship was immeasurably rewarding for me and noticeably happy for her — until her life was cruelly cut short at what should have been its midpoint. She was only seven and a half. Well-cared-for pet cats can easily live to age 15 and longer.

Back to the beginning — that February afternoon in 1975 at the ASPCA shelter. As I strolled around the room where the cats were housed, Lucy's was the first cage that tempted me to stop for a longer look. There was something about her pert demeanor and delicate beauty — gleaming black poured randomly over white — that reminded me of a dainty Victorian doll in an old-fashioned picture book. She sat poised upright, like an Egyptian cat goddess, and peered winsomely at me through the bars. When I reached in a couple of fingers to stroke her cheek she purred loudly. When I opened the cage and gathered her up for an introductory hug, she snuggled against me with needy urgency.

That was that. My decision was made on the spot. This slender, adoring teenager with the green eyes and the jet-button nose was coming home with me. All that remained to do was the adoption paperwork. And — not least — the selection of a *second* cat to come along with her and keep both of us company.

To complete my "starter set" I was obliged to choose a female. The ASPCA management wouldn't release two cats of different sexes into the same home if neither had yet been neutered. (Back then, their policy required adopters to pay a deposit toward a pet's spay-neuter surgery in their clinic, to be scheduled later. Nowadays, few well-run shelters anywhere in the country allow a sexually mature pet to leave the premises *un*sterilized.) So while Lucy waited back in her cage, reserved for me, I perused the other available females at some length. Finally, the cat I would name Rosalie emerged as the best choice. She was about the same age as Lucy, beautiful in a strikingly different way, and appeared friendly if not overtly affectionate. You'll hear all about her in the next chapter.

What did the ASPCA know about Lucy's background? She was estimated to be just under a year old — from the last season's kitten crop — and had been turned in as a pet, not a stray. She'd been brought to the shelter about two weeks earlier by someone who gave "10 Catherine Street" as an address and "can't keep" as the reason for surrendering her.

(A full year later, while on a shopping errand to Manhattan's Lower East Side, I tried to locate the home where my little love's life had begun. Sort of a pilgrimage. It turned out that no "Catherine Street" existed. There was, however, an address named Catherine *Slip* — where cargo ships used to moor in the old days. No. 10 was a huge public-housing project, with several buildings that might have dated from the Depression, in a predominantly Puerto Rican neighborhood. No way, obviously, to find Lucy's first owner here. I spied some boys playing ball in the yard and asked one if the families who lived in these apartments were allowed to keep pets. His answer was "no." So I concocted my own scenario: A young resident here found a black-and-white kitten, took her in and cared for her, until sternly informed that "you can't keep that cat." And that young person loved her enough to make the long tedious trip all the way uptown to the ASPCA shelter, trusting they would find her a good, safe, permanent home. That was my fantasy, anyway.)

When I arrived home with Lucy and Rosalie, my apartment had been readied to welcome them. Food and water dishes in the kitchen, litter box in the bathroom, a few toys scattered about, plenty of cushiony seats to curl up on. My new companions reacted exactly the way I had hoped, a few weeks earlier, that the unfortunate Kiowa and Janis would behave. For a half-hour or so they prowled the premises, exploring and sniffing in every room. Then, having satisfied their curiosity and got their bearings, they settled side by side atop a chest of drawers and looked at me expectantly, as if saying "OK; now what?"

My rapport with Lucy was instant, total and magical. (I can't remember exactly when I decided on her name but it was early and easy — just right for her.) We were each other's Number One from day one. The first night, as I stretched out on my stomach to sleep, she settled down on the small of my back. Is this what she'd been used to in her earlier home? Though she didn't weigh much I found it uncomfortable. So I rolled over, picked her up and placed her firmly down at the foot of my bed. This sequence of movements was then repeated a half-dozen times. Finally, when I lay down once again, I felt her approach from the foot of the bed and curl up *next to my side.* Success! Once learned, the lesson held. Later, she developed an endearing habit of crawling under the covers on chilly nights and snuggling cozily against my midsection.

Little Lucy was fragile at first. She was timid, underweight with a meager appetite, hypersensitive to bright light. She and Rosalie had both contracted an upper-respiratory infection while at the ASPCA. Lucy developed such a nasty cold that she couldn't smell her food — therefore wouldn't eat. I tried giving her children's nose drops to open her nasal passages. Clumsily, I held her over a steaming hot bathtub to inhale the therapeutic vapor. *That* ended with her fall into the scalding water, then a frantic towel rubdown.

With time, T.L.C. worked its wonders. As soon as the cats had recovered enough from their colds to undergo surgery, both were spayed. Good medical care, along with a nutritious diet and a stable, comfortable home, strengthened Lucy appreciably. She gradually grew sturdy and sleek, while remaining no less dainty and lovely.

She and Rosalie developed a nice sisterly relationship. This served them especially well when the two were packed together in a single pet carrier for the long ride to and from our country quarters on weekends. They would doze off and on through the four-hour trip, with Rosalie's tongue bestowing an occasional soothing wash on Lucy's head. In the house, they often lounged near each other without actually touching. When they played chasing games, Lucy was always the initiator and pursuer.

Though she never lost her shyness with strangers, Lucy's attachment to me grew firmer every day. She had the rare quality of empathy — a gift for sensing and sharing another's feelings — that we more often hear attributed to pet dogs than to cats. Once, I remember, I came home upset by a hurtful argument with a friend. As I sat with my face buried in my hands, weeping, I felt my head being gently nudged. There perched next to me was Lucy, caressing me with a look of quizzical concern. (Anthropomorphism! You hear me ascribing human behavior to an animal — and not for the last time, either.)

A memorable moment of stress when she again sought to comfort me was when I learned of my father's death. Though far from unexpected (as mentioned earlier, he had long suffered from emphysema), the news was still a shock — most palpably, to my digestive system. During the night I was aroused several times by a call of nature. Each time I returned to bed, Lucy crept back under the covers to settle her warm, loyal little self firmly against my shivering stomach. Later that same year, while I was convalescing from surgery and needed lengthy and frequent naps, she rarely left my side.

For their first couple of years with me, Lucy and Rosalie were commuter cats. They spent weekdays confined to a tenth-floor city apartment, left to their own devices during working hours except when I was able to stop home at lunchtime. Most weekends and summer vacations, they accompanied me to the country. There, dressed with collars and identification tags, they were introduced to the indoor-outdoor life.

Then, on Memorial Day weekend in 1977, their lives were transformed: they became full-time country cats. No more tedious back-and-forth travels by taxi, subway, railroad and car! Just *one* home now — for all of us! I had quit my job in the city. I never accepted another, though I had a few interviews, and never again was tempted to live in town. From my new base in the country I recycled myself into a self-employed new life as freelance writer and advertising consultant.

Both cats adapted happily to the change. Rosalie, the more intrepid of the two, had more adventures and mishaps and caused me more worry; you'll hear about all this later. Lucy's only two misadventures were during her very first summer, while we were still weekending in a rented cottage. One day she got lost deep in the woods behind the house; a sustained campaign of calling and clapping eventually brought her back out. The second time she disappeared, I searched and called throughout the neighborhood in vain. I was getting frantic when someone suggested looking in the crawl basement. We lifted the old-fashioned cellar door — and sure enough! She raced up the steps to safety. I never learned just how she had fallen down there, but the heavy door was too thick to let us hear her trapped cries from below.

Once settled in our permanent new home, Lucy's existence was reassuringly uneventful. Aside from treatment for one poisonous insect bite, her medical record was sparse. She adhered faithfully to my safety guidelines for indoor-outdoor pets, to wit: Always *inside the house at night.* During daylight hours, the weather and my own schedule permitting, the cats are allowed out after their breakfast. I expect them back indoors at dinner-time or darkness, whichever comes first. The system has worked pretty well because the cats are served their meals at set times — no free self-feeding! — so the dinner call normally proves an irresistible lure.

I can't remember Lucy ever arriving home late for her evening meal. Nor did she fail to respond when she was called back inside because of darkness, rain or snow. She was usually within earshot of my whistle and would come cantering eagerly across the lawn to land with a flying leap on the back stoop. Nor do I recall seeing her ever cross the road in front of our house, with its speeding traffic, to explore the other side. She seemed perfectly content to play and hunt and entertain herself on the safe side of the street, in our own spacious yard and the properties of our nearest neighbors. She had ample woods, fields and underbrush to prowl through and abundant small prey to stalk. One of her preferred hangouts was under a Japanese black pine tree, next to the bird-bath. She'd spend hours resting there on the pine-needle carpet, watching for birds to pounce on — but they, of course, would steer clear of the bath until she had gone.

So Lucy's life went on, pleasantly and predictably, up to the second week of October in 1981.

It was glorious early-fall weather, the most beautiful time of year on eastern Long Island. I was busy planting bulbs in my garden. Lucy, when not hunting mice, hung around lazily to keep me company. (The saying "I love work; I can watch it for hours" may well have been coined by the owner of another spectator cat.) But something odd was happening. All that week, for the first time ever, she seemed reluctant to come indoors at the end of the day. On two or three evenings I even had to go out into the yard, find her, pick her up, and carry her into the house. Once, as I did so, she actually *growled*. At night, inside, she was her usual relaxed and affectionate self. What was going on?

Over the long Columbus Day weekend I had house guests staying with me. Sunday, October 11th was a picture-perfect day. Late that afternoon, as my guests and I arrived back home from an excursion, Lucy was sitting in a flower bed next to the driveway. I reached out to her for a hug after we parked the car — but she turned away and trotted off into the woods. A bit later, I called her in for dinner before my guests and I went out for the evening. She was nearby but refused to come. Through a window I caught a last glimpse of her, cavorting under a tree in the brisk autumn breeze. The sun had just set; a full moon was rising. Well, I thought, I can't delay our own plans indefinitely while I try to lure Lucy into the house. If she insists on staying out a while longer on this gorgeous evening — it'll be an interesting new experience for her. And we'll be back in a few hours.

My visitors and I had a delightful outing: an excellent restaurant dinner followed by an entertaining show at the local theatre. It wasn't late when we returned home. As the car slowed to a stop, the bright full moon revealed a small shape on the driveway, lying just outside the screen door to the porch. It was Lucy. Her head was battered; her body was stiffening. Evidently she'd had enough strength to drag herself as far as the house before collapsing. Had she expected to find me there waiting for her? How long had she agonized, alone, until she died? No more than a minute or so, I fervently hoped.

The shock was indescribable. Somehow I got through the night, having left Lucy on the locked screen porch to await burial. First thing next morning I dug a grave in her favorite spot under the Japanese black pine. In a pillowcase from my bed, topped with a freshly cut rose, she was placed in her final home. Then I went inside for breakfast with my guests — close relatives of mine. They departed early, helpless to mitigate my distress.

The ensuing days and weeks were a blur. I existed on an emotional roller coaster. I actually placed a display ad in the town weekly, asking the driver of the car that had hit a black-and-white cat on my street that Sunday night to phone and tell me how it happened — no names needed, no questions asked. Naturally, no one responded. My ad was a foolish waste of money. Any *compassionate* motorist would immediately have stopped to help the stricken pet, then managed to contact me via the phone number on the ID tag she wore. I had evidence of this kind behavior on later occasions, after accidents with other pets.

I placed a pink flagstone on Lucy's grave. A year or so later, when I learned of a firm specializing in the work, I ordered a simple metal plaque engraved with her name and dates and my farewell tribute. Now, all the cats resting in my garden cemetery — nine at the present writing — have similar plaques affixed to their pink gravestones.

My bereavement elicited the same sympathy from friends as if I had lost a child. (Later, I'll deal a bit with comparisons of our attachment to pets and to children: how do the relationships resemble and differ from each other?) In Lucy's memorial album, which I inaugurated with her photos, no less than seven condolence notes are filed. "Losing an animal is even worse than losing a person," wrote one friend, "because with an animal you have only *good* memories." Previously, I had lost two persons I cared for very much. But Lucy was the first living being I had loved *and* shared a home with continuously, every day, for years. Because I loved her the most, her loss was the worst. Yet there was one consoling thought: no future bereavement could ever be as hard to bear!

For a long time I thought about Lucy every day and dreamed about her many nights. *And* I wrote to her, exhaustively. My letters, a survivor's journal, fill 35 single-spaced pages. The first two years they poured thick and fast from my typewriter, each time I was vividly reminded of my lost love. Then, I settled into writing her an annual letter on the anniversary of her death, or as close to it as I could manage. One year I found myself strolling through downtown Bratislava, capital of the Slovak Republic, when I suddenly realized it was the 11th of October. I thought about my Lucy while I continued sightseeing in that remote setting. As soon as I came home I composed my memorial message, giving her the year's household news. My last letter to her was in 2001 — a full 20 years after she left me.

Two questions preoccupied me throughout these long-winded missives. One — should pet cats ever be allowed free access to the outdoors? — is a vital decision for every owner and, of course, a controversial issue. I want to review the pros and cons in detail but prefer to reserve this for later.

The other problem I obsessed over is epitomized by the Biblical lament, "Why hast thou forsaken me?" *What* had impelled Lucy to abandon her longtime home and habits and pursue her strange self-destructive course? From the meanderings in my letters:

> *"Why were you on the road for — as best I know — the very first time in your six years of country living? Were you driven berserk by the strange night and moonlight? Were you tracking a rabbit?"*

"I'm now quite convinced that your death resulted from a definite — if maybe temporary — personality change. You were drunk with the sudden, great discovery of the night hunting excitement under an autumn full moon. You were driven by that too-quickly-acquired passion to a reckless disregard of the enemies you had prudently respected for six years."

"I've now come around to feeling that you in effect committed suicide. Perhaps driven by that wild, irrational I-want-to-stay-OUT-and-hunt-and-have-adventures impulse, you lost all control and judgment. There were 43,000 square feet of home territory, plus neighboring safe woods and brush, where you could have played and hunted that night — but you were driven toward mortal temptations on a few feet of road."

"I've come to convince myself that your bizarre pre-suicide behavior was some kind of medical aberration, not just moon-looniness. Maybe a little brain fever or a mini-tumor? Some chemical change? I know this can happen to anyone, anytime."

And so on. It occurred to me that I could consult an animal behaviorist for a professional opinion on Lucy's sudden transformation. But I feared this would only rub salt in my wounds — and yield nothing more than expert speculation. What analyst, after all, is equipped to second-guess the mental state of a deceased animal?

One night on TV, a few years after Lucy died, I watched an anniversary tribute to the Beatles' classic "Sergeant Pepper" album. When a verse from their song "Lucy in the Sky with Diamonds" was played, the picture of a cat floated across my screen! The next night I wrote to Lucy:

"That's how I think of you sometimes, my darling: not the 'acid' LSD, but the lovely drifting and dancing forever up there among the stars. As they glittered the night we said goodbye."

But the commemorative quote that suits her best is from a poem by William Wordsworth. It headlines a montage of my favorite photos of her that hangs on the wall next to my bed:

"She lived unknown, and few could know
When Lucy ceased to be;
But she is in her grave, and, oh,
The difference to me!"

6

Rosalie

Gorgeous Egotist

Every pet rates a superlative — whether or not the *mot juste* comes quickly to mind — and Rosalie might be called my best-looking cat. She would, at least, have tied for top place in a beauty contest with Daisy May (who didn't come along until two decades later).

Cat-fancy professionals would describe Rosalie as a pastel or brindled calico. Meaning, the classic calico's three distinct coat colors — red, white and black — had been whipped by genetic blender into a purée of pink and gray and creamy beige, with lots of white on her underside. Another common variant of calico is tortoiseshell: here, red and black predominate in the mix for a streaked brownish-gold coat. Molly, one of my present cats, is indeed colored like a tortoiseshell comb. "Calico" is a pattern, not a breed. All calico cats are random-bred domestic shorthairs or longhairs — and virtually all are female.

Rosalie was a lot lovelier than the "mushed-up calico" I often used to describe her. The rosy-pink streaks through her coat inspired her name. A bit younger than Lucy, she had an enchanting still-kittenish face. Whoever turned her in to the ASPCA had specified her age as 10 months; presumably they'd known her since birth. The reason given for surrender was "moving," from an address, like Lucy's, on the Lower East Side of Manhattan.

A year later, the same day I tracked down Lucy's first home while on an errand in the area, I also visited the house on Essex Street where Rosalie's original family had lived. It was a seedy six-story tenement with spray-can graffiti plastering the entrance hall and no names visible on the mailboxes. In bygone days the neighborhood must have been home to Jewish immigrants; an old Hebrew school was still standing across the street. But now the shops and pedestrians indicated that a largely Puerto Rican and black population had taken over. Whatever demographic group Rosalie's first owners belonged to, and for whatever reason they couldn't take her with them when they moved, I was delighted that she had graduated to a gentrified new life uptown.

From the outset she was a curious, intrepid little explorer. Even while confined to our tenth-floor city apartment, months before she started going to the country on weekends, she needed an identification tag attached to her collar. Every time the front door was opened, Rosalie shot out into the hallway to explore all along the corridor and sniff under the neighbors' doors. Now and then, the door to the fire stairs would be propped open by the maintenance staff or tenants depositing trash on the landing. My nightmare was that one day Rosalie might disappear into that inviting stairwell — to emerge on a totally different floor of the building where no one, of course, would know her. Luckily this never happened. But for my peace of mind, she and Lucy were given metal ID tags engraved with my name and phone number so that their home could be easily contacted

Here, I should note that I'm a fanatic on the importance of pet identification — indoor as well as outdoor pets. I've harangued other owners to the point of nuisance on this subject, especially cat owners. Dog owners, though often lax, are still more inclined to equip their pets with some kind of label, such as a license or rabies-vaccination tag.

Once turned loose outside the city, Rosalie's real adventures began. Both she and Lucy took quickly and easily to country life. They prowled the woods and fields and underbrush. They learned to run up and down trees and sharpen their claws on the bark — thereby helping to extend the life of the indoor scratching post their mom had invested in. They got used to relieving themselves outdoors — again, helpfully sparing mom some maintenance of the indoor litter box. Both became adept predators and triumphantly toted home their kill — voles, moles, chipmunks, the occasional bird — for mom to get rid of.

I remember the Sunday morning I discovered not one but two dead mice lying just outside the back door. I was heading toward the woods, gingerly carrying a rodent corpse by its tail in each rubber-gloved hand, as two neatly dressed ladies with benevolent smiles came walking up my driveway. Bible missionaries! I graciously smiled back with a shrug as I displayed my unsightly cargo. They instantly spun around and left.

Another time, Rosalie and Lucy managed to bring a live baby rabbit indoors to toy with. After rescuing the terrified creature from under my office radiator, I vowed never again to leave a door open even briefly for free feline access into or out of the house. (And forget about those cunning little "pet flaps" cut into doors!) There are plenty of good reasons for this rule. But the disposal of unsavory hunting trophies always heads my own list.

One of Rosalie's early country adventures rated a short article (unpublished) by her writer mom. On a raw, gray Sunday afternoon in late November she decided to explore a Really Tall oak tree in the adjoining woods. Up, up and away she went. Eventually, finding herself stranded on a swaying branch 30 feet above ground, she began to wail piteously without pause. I stood below calling her repeatedly and lovingly. Impossible to entice her down. In a few hours I would have to close up the house and get us all on the train back to the city. *What* to do?

Are firemen actually willing to climb their huge ladders to rescue cats stuck in trees? Only one way to find out. When I phoned the local fire department, just a mile down the road, a couple of volunteer firemen were sitting around doing nothing much on an uneventful Sunday. "In our experience, ma'am," the man who answered assured me, "the cat eventually comes down from the tree." I assured *him* that I understood this — but unfortunately couldn't afford to wait for "eventually" or I'd miss work the next day.

Soon, a small fire truck pulled into my driveway. They'd notified the deputy fire chief, at home, and he was intrigued enough to tear himself away from his TV. (Was he perhaps a cat fancier? I never asked.) Up went the tall ladder against Rosalie's oak. She looked on with interest, barely interrupting her heartrending cries. The deputy chief, a short and nimble man, worked his way slowly upward until Rosalie was within reach. He managed to carry her part of the way down clutched to his shoulder. Then she leaped free, crash-landed on the ground and sped away. The firemen and I cheered. Later I mailed a generous donation, with my thanks, to their department's fireworks fund.

There was an illuminating sequel. Months later, one beautiful summer evening, Rosalie got herself stuck up *another* tree. Again I could hear her plaintive cries. I could also glimpse her silhouette against the full moon on the rise. Her problem, as before, was that I had been clipping the tips of her claws to save wear and tear on my furniture. So her best way to descend — bottom first rather than head first — was handicapped by an inability to get a good grip into the tree bark as she worked her way each step down. But I couldn't reach her, or even hang around to wait for her "eventual" descent. My house guest and I were on our way out to the movies. Worried about my stranded pet, I couldn't enjoy the film much. Yet my friend kept reassuring me that Rosalie would manage just fine. And sure enough: there she was at the door to greet us when we arrived home. *She had learned!*

But Rosalie also learned to stay out late after it got dark, well past the dinner call, and to explore areas beyond our property where she might get into trouble. I was particularly nervous about the road in front of our house. Though not a major thoroughfare, the cars were frequent and fast enough to leave plenty of squirrel and possum roadkills. Could I possibly "train" Rosalie to avoid the street?

One day she sauntered up to join me while I was pruning roses at the front fence. I decided to try scaring her *away* from the traffic. I picked her up, held her firmly, and screamed a loud, menacing "No!" into her ear each time a car drove by. The idea was that she'd automatically associate the sight and sound of a vehicle with a nasty, frightening noise. My notion of aversion conditioning may have been way off base. But remember, I was still pretty much of a novice at keeping cats and understanding their psychology. At any rate, my intimidation tactic seems to have worked. I rarely saw Rosalie venture into the street and, until the very end, she had no encounters with cars.

On another occasion I innocently set out to entertain Rosalie with a new adventure — but managed instead to terrify her. Early one summer evening, while it was still daylight but the crowds had left the beach, I drove her down to the ocean. I released her from her cat carrier on the sand near the water's edge. The breaking surf was thundering, a brisk breeze was blowing — and there was absolutely nowhere in that huge, empty expanse of sand and sea and sky for a bewildered little cat to take cover. Petrified, Rosalie fled all the way back up the beach and disappeared into the dunes. It took the better part of a half-hour for her to heed my calls and be enticed safely back to the car and into her carrier.

Of course I hadn't meant to be cruel. But I had yet to learn that most cats, unlike most dogs, do *not* like the beach. Why? They *hate* the noise, the wind and the lack of protective cover — and don't much care for the water either. Once, years later, I did encounter a couple of beachgoers walking a very small black pet on a leash along the sand. Approaching, I thought it looked like a toy poodle puppy. But no, it was a cat — and a wet cat at that. They told me she enjoyed short dips at the surf edge and, later, relaxing under a little umbrella tent next to them while they sunbathed. The exception that proves the rule!

Rosalie had an unpredictable, complex personality. She was

very bright and independent-minded and resourceful — what the French call *débrouillarde*, capable of working out the best solution for herself in most situations. Yet she could also be neurotically skittish and jittery, an easily spooked "scaredy cat." She had her egotistical moments as a willful and self-indulgent prima donna — and her gentle, vulnerable moments as the sweetest of cuddlecats. She showed affection with compulsive kneading and slurping (a frequent carryover from nursing kittenhood). Moreover, I'm convinced she had a sense of fun. My last snapshot of her shows her favorite "dopey Rosie" mode: lying on her back, feet in air, staring dumbly at the camera, in a take-me-I'm-yours pose of helpless surrender.

Her medical record was minimal. Shortly after adoption she went into heat. She hadn't yet recovered enough from the respiratory infection she picked up at the shelter to undergo spay surgery. For a week she squirmed and rubbed and chirped and sweated her way around the apartment. (At least she didn't emit the ear-splitting shrieks that my erstwhile lodger, the blue-point Siamese, had so unnerved me with.) Of course there were no tomcats around to satisfy Rosalie's mating urge. But Lucy instinctively sensed her sister's need and — as I watched with amusement — would helpfully mount and massage her from time to time to relieve her tension.

Once spayed, nothing much bothered Rosalie beyond stomach upsets. She was inclined to gluttony, as many cats are, and often gulped her food too fast to digest it properly. But for more than six years her visits to the vet remained routine. Then, in the summer and fall of 1981, she developed an eye infection followed by a liver inflammation. The latter involved exploratory surgery — a stressful time for me as well as the patient, since it was only a week after my catastrophic loss of Lucy. Rosalie's treatment was lengthy and costly but she responded well. Ironically, by the time she was shipshape again she had only weeks left to live.

What drove Rosalie to a premature end was, I think, the fearful streak in her nature. Despite her success as intrepid explorer and skilled hunter, despite her relaxed friendliness and easy acceptance of unfamiliar people and animals, a nervous "flight reflex" was embedded in her soul. It surfaced most visibly after Tim joined our family. (You'll hear all about him a bit later.) For the nearly full year they shared a home, Rosalie never trusted Tim *not* to switch from innocent play to predatory attack. He was absolutely harmless: a big, shaggy, easygoing hunk who cherished his comfort and bore not an iota of ill will toward man or beast. Yet he and Rosalie quickly developed a pattern. He would tease; she would protest. He would pursue; she would flee. He was always the "hunter;" she was always the "prey." Their typical evening game — which *she* might initiate by starting to run — would often end with Tim chasing Rosalie into the linen closet. There, she'd settle down cozily on a pile of Turkish towels while he went back to his own preferred snoozing spot. All good fun and perfectly safe until the day their game turned deadly.

It was a brilliantly clear, icy cold afternoon in early February 1982. I was meeting with an advertising client in my home office when the front doorbell rang. A young woman stood there; Tim was beside her and dashed into the house. She asked if I owned another, multicolored cat that she had just hit with her car. Apparently the cat appeared twice as she was driving down my street. Rosalie had first emerged from the underbrush on the other side and crossed the road *toward* my front yard. There, a second cat (Tim) was visible who started toward her. Rosalie had then wheeled *away* from the yard, raced back into the road and slammed into the car. The driver braked but couldn't avoid her.

As we talked on the doorstep, Rosalie had come back to collapse a few feet from the house. Suddenly she emitted a long, sharp, loud groan (her death cry?). The car's compassionate driver, a nurse, offered to chauffeur me and my pet to the veterinarian. Hoping against hope, I placed Rosalie's motionless body in her carrier. But the doctor waiting for us at the hospital confirmed immediately that she was gone.

I had to leave her there to be cremated. The ground was frozen too hard to dig a grave for her. Two weeks later, though, it had thawed enough to bury Rosalie's ashes close to Lucy's resting place. Goodbye to my first generation of long-term, full-time pets! Both of my little ASPCA ladies, who joined my home the same day, had been killed in the road four months apart. Our family trio, so close-knit for so long, was now shattered. Rosalie, if she'd lived three more weeks, would have been my pet exactly seven years.

Her gravestone plaque reads "My gorgeous Rosalie." Again, I received condolence notes from friends. Again, I wrote letters to my departed pet ("Rosabelle, my beautiful cuddlecat" etc.). While appreciative and affectionate, they weren't as long or as frequent as my farewell letters to Lucy: just five and a half pages in all, up until the tenth anniversary. I put it honestly in my first-anniversary message to Rosalie: "With some guilt and discomfiture, I must confess that I did not miss you for very long after you died. Something to do with the kind of relationship you and I had, I suppose."

Quite simply, it paled beside the relationship I'd had with Lucy. The two bereavements taught me how greatly our attachment to individual pets can vary.

I felt morally obliged to reexamine my indoor-outdoor policy. Two cherished cats had already been road-killed. A third, Tim, had been hit by a car too, but he managed to survive with a damaged jaw, minus several teeth and a piece of his tongue. While the veterinary bill was a pain for me, the punishing cost for Tim was having to eat very, very slowly for the rest of his days. So I agonized:

Should I play it safe from now on and keep my pets confined entirely inside the house? (Of course, the indoor life would be my cats' *only* option if we still lived in a city apartment or any home in a highly dangerous neighborhood. But this didn't happen to be the case.) Should I train them to walk on leashes like little dogs? Should I build some kind of fenced and roofed fresh-air enclosure that would allow them access to the outdoors — but without the dangerous freedom to roam? These elaborate and expensive structures are vigorously promoted in the pet-care literature.

Or, should I take my chances on the existing system, with its prudent restrictions and proven risks, and hope for the best? My cats can enjoy outdoor liberty during *daylight hours only*, each day's weather and my own schedule permitting. Naturally, they are *always* spayed and neutered, *always* up-to-date on their vaccinations (including outdoor-contracted diseases like rabies), and *always* clearly identified as my pets with my name and phone number.

Note that even cautious permissiveness like mine runs counter to the advice of most veterinarians and humane professionals. Earnestly and tirelessly, they urge owners to keep our cats safely inside their homes. I appreciate their solicitude and respect their motives. But I do resent the patronizing assumptions some advocates of the indoor-only lifestyle make about owners like me. We are, they imply, ignorant of the dangers awaiting our pets outdoors — or uncaring about their security and well-being.

Not so! We don't need repeated reminders of all the threats

awaiting the free-roaming cat: speeding cars, attacking animals, disease-carrying insects, parasite-infested rodents, toxic lawn chemicals, lethal antifreeze, careless hunters, thoughtless strangers, sheds and pools and cellars and hidden enclosures that can so easily entrap an exploring pet…. We've already learned many of these lessons the hard way. But more important, I care far too much about my pets' pleasure to keep them confined. For me, the *quality* of their lives takes precedence over sheer longevity.

All cat lovers who share this priority want our pets to enjoy the best of both worlds. We also hope they'll survive safely to a ripe old age (as so many unconfined cats I've known do). But if an indoor-outdoor cat's life happens to be unluckily cut short — well, we can take comfort in remembering that it was a happy, varied and fulfilling life. Lucy's certainly was. Rosalie's too.

So, back three decades ago, I didn't have to weigh the pros and cons for long. I made a gut decision, once and for all, that *every* cat of mine would be able to savor the joys and risks of free time outdoors.

7

Casey

A Litter Box Lesson

Here, let's backtrack a bit. I've been introducing my cats to you in the chronological order that they joined the household. In a multi-cat home like mine, arrivals and departures are bound to overlap. Pet C, for example, may already have come and gone, and a new Pet D settled in, while starter Pets A and B are still on the scene. After either A or B goes, the next to fill a vacancy will be Pet E…and so on.

Casey, my Pet C, fit into this pattern with a very brief stay. He was one of my two conspicuous failures.

By November 1980, Lucy and Rosalie and I had been living as a contented nuclear family for five years and nine months. I felt it might add some spice and fun to bring home a new sibling for them. Preferably a little brother. A fellow volunteer in my local humane group offered an appealing candidate. She'd been caring for a stray neighborhood momcat with a litter of orange-tabby kittens, then about eight weeks old. I don't recall if Casey was the last one available for adoption or simply the cutest, but he suited me to a T. His youth, his gender, his coloring, his feisty-yet-cuddly personality all made for a good, complementary fit with my long-established girls approaching middle age.

Naturally, Lucy and Rosalie weren't overjoyed to see him. As I used to remind visitors at the animal shelter when I volunteered as an adoption counselor, no resident feline has ever been known to extend a "Welcome! I'm so glad to have you here" greeting to a newcomer. Cats are, after all, among the most territorially possessive of animals. Lucy, according to a note in my diary, actually went on a hunger strike for a day or so. But it quickly became clear that the new little boy posed no threat whatever to his big sisters' secure place in my home and affections. Soon they were all getting along nicely.

Casey's name stemmed from an old song, and a 1940's movie featuring it, about the redheaded Irish in turn-of-the-20th-century New York: "Casey would waltz with a strawberry blonde, and the band played on…." My own Casey waltzed happily around the house, having free run of the premises after being kept a few initial days in the guest room. While he had his individual food dish in the kitchen, he shared the same litter box in the bathroom that Lucy and Rosalie used. Since both girls spent much of the day outdoors in good weather, they didn't need the box often. Casey, still confined indoors due to his tender age and the advent of winter, had the feline toilet facilities pretty much to himself.

For a couple of months everything was fine. Then, Casey began to misbehave. I couldn't call the episodes "accidents." He had full control of his functions — but chose deliberately to defecate outside his box. (Yet he continued to urinate where he was supposed to, in the litter.) Once or twice I actually saw him dig a hole in the litter, circle it, then step *out* of the box to leave his deposit on the bathroom rug. Under my very eyes!

What on earth was going on? I encouraged him, gently but firmly, to step in and stay in the box until mission accomplished, and praised him effusively whenever he performed properly. He didn't create a mess every day. But it happened regularly enough for me to start wondering how long I'd be able to put up with it — and with him.

Animal behaviorists call this activity "house soiling" or "inappropriate elimination." In each case we need to find the cause. Is it a verifiable medical condition, such as a gastric or bladder ailment? Is it a mechanical problem, such as a litter box that is dirty, smelly, hard to access or lacking in privacy? If these can all be thoroughly checked and then ruled out, the explanation has to be psychological. The deliberately misbehaving cat is Making a Statement. The challenge for his owner is to interpret the message. What exactly was Casey trying to tell me?

One night at the end of February, around 2 AM, I was awakened by a soft rattling sound. I turned on the bedside lamp and immediately saw a small pile of dung on the rug in front of my dresser. The floppy metal handles of the dresser drawers click when touched or dropped. Presumably this is how Casey had aroused my attention, *after* depositing his message and disappearing from the room.

That was the moment of truth. I cleaned the rug and went back to bed. First thing next morning I phoned my veterinary hospital to reserve a boarding cage for Casey. Then, I called my humane group (which hadn't yet built its own shelter) and officially listed him for adoption. I made no mention to anyone of his litter box behavior, saying just that the arrangement in my own home "hadn't worked out."

After giving Casey his breakfast I packed him off to his new veterinary quarters. Boarding would, of course, be at my expense. If he wasn't adopted into a good, permanent new home after two or three months, I was prepared to authorize euthanasia.

He had been my pet for exactly 100 days.

To my relief, Casey found a new family very quickly. A divorced father in a mobile home who shared custody of his child wanted a suitable indoor cat for both of them. Casey was their sole pet, he had a litter box entirely to himself, and the humane office heard no further news of him. Obviously, I like to think he lived happily ever after.

With hindsight, I realize that I could probably have solved my problem with Casey very easily. My male kitten, now growing up, needed some "space" of his own. And I, now housing three cats, needed an additional litter box. The lesson belatedly learned, I installed a second box for the arrival of Tim — my Pet D.

8

Tim

Who Dumped Me

Timbo, as I chose to call him in chummier moments, was not just striking but spectacular to look on.

My only longhaired cat, ever, wore his luxuriant coat with consummate style. The softest creamy-white silk, accented with gray, ended in a magnificent dark bush of a tail. The gaze from his big yellow eyes suggested modest intelligence, at best, and a detached view of his fellow creatures and the world. He turned out to be quite a high-maintenance pet — and not just because of all that long, ultrafine hair.

He appeared in my life at the beginning of March 1981. It was a day or so after I'd banished the incorrigible Casey to a boarding cage at the vet's to be put up for adoption elsewhere. Learning of my new vacancy, a fellow volunteer in our humane group suggested I try Tim as a foster pet for a while: see how well he meshed with my long-resident Lucy and Rosalie. No problem! After two weeks of his easygoing and highly decorative company, I decided he fit in fine and was happy to make the adoption official.

As with so many rescued strays, Tim's origins were a mystery. He'd been discovered at Christmastime 1979 "hanging around" a local supermarket; he was then judged to be about a year old. It was clear, from his trusting and friendly behavior, that he hadn't lived as a feral cat remote from people or been seriously mistreated by anyone. Most likely he'd been someone's pet, casually cared for and indifferently supervised, who simply got lost — or managed to hitch a ride on a vehicle that carried him away from his home territory.

He spent the next year or so in a home boarding facility used by the humane group. There, I think, he acquired the name "Tim." The group may have advertised him as a "found" pet, but no one came forward to claim him — and no owner ever seems to have advertised for his return as a "missing" pet. So he was still young, just over two years, by the time he joined my household.

Early on, he had a bad collision with a car. A neighbor of mine found him sitting dazed at the side of the road, lower jaw all mangled and bloody. I gingerly lifted him into a carrier and alerted the animal hospital, a half-hour's drive away, to expect his emergency arrival. The doctor performed wonders. But even after he'd saved and expertly stitched up my battered pet, Tim would never be good as new. Minus several teeth and a portion of his tongue, he was obliged to eat very, very slowly for the rest of his life. His accident did have one constructive result. Though he continued to cross the street when the spirit moved him, Tim's trauma apparently taught him to be wary enough of traffic so that he never had a close encounter again.

Grooming my hirsute pet was part pleasure, part pain. Like most cats, he loved being rhythmically stroked with a rubber brush or mitt; then having the loosened fur gently lifted off with a fine-toothed comb. The less pleasant moments, unfortunately not rare, were after impenetrable mats of hair had formed. These had to be carefully disentangled, involving nasty yanks by me and plaintive yelps from Tim. Sometimes I just took a sharp scissors from my sewing box and cut off the whole offending snarl. This runs counter to prevailing pet-care advice. In theory, only professional groomers are qualified for such delicate barbering jobs; in practice, my amateur home clipping sufficed.

Yet my biggest maintenance challenge wasn't Timbo's tangled fur. It was his allergic skin, which reacted angrily to flea bites. Only one other of all my cats, Lucky, suffered from this acute sensitivity, which afflicts dogs more commonly than cats. The symptoms go well beyond scratching at a site where some little bugger bit. Poor Tim would scrape and chew off chunks of his hair to leave raw inflamed patches, especially on his lower back just above the tail. Mind you, this was years before any of today's effective pest controls, like Frontline and Advantage, had appeared on the market. The main preventive available then was the medicated flea collar. I never liked to use these, partly because their insecticide was so toxic, partly because it meant burdening my small pets with a second neckpiece added to their tagged ID collars. In Tim's case, however, I had to make an exception.

As for treating the flea-allergy dermatitis itself, the worst out-breaks required a prescription for strong anti-inflammatory med-ication (cortisone), administered orally. Even in the coldest winter months, when all fleas had vanished outdoors, Tim had to be protected from the *indoor* menace: flea larvae emerging from eggs which had been laid during the warm season in the cozy recesses of my upholstered furniture and rugs. This necessitated a ritual I performed on a clear cold day every December for as long as Tim (and later, Lucky) lived in my home:

First, all cats were shooed out of the house — into my heated basement if the outdoor temperature was too icy. Next, I made sure that all closet and cabinet doors and dresser drawers were left open and all windows securely shut. Then, armed with an insecticidal spray formula purchased at the vet's, I emptied the contents of the can throughout the house before exiting myself. (Premises larger than my 1,200-square-foot single-story house would, of course, have required two or more bombs.) The lethal fog was left to do its work for an hour or longer. Then, I returned to open wide the windows and air the place thoroughly before letting my animals back inside.

As you'd imagine, this annual chore for the benefit of just one pet was never a date I looked forward to. Not least, I had to devise some productive outdoor activity to keep myself warm, like leaf raking or brush clearing, while waiting out the fumigation pe-riod. But every year it paid off handsomely. For the remainder of the winter Tim remained dependably free of fleas and his tender skin free of blemishes.

Of course I couldn't begrudge my big beautiful boy the special treatment. He was such a luxury to look at and touch, such an amiable companion. In moments of unbridled pleasure — say, when being lovingly stroked — he'd drool like a happy puppy.

He got along nicely with his siblings, though he did have an impulse to spook Rosalie now and then. (He would playfully pursue; she would frantically flee. As noted earlier, this may have provoked her final, fatal encounter with a car.) Easygoing and undemanding, he seemed content with his life — which makes his decision to walk out on his home all the more puzzling.

The strange behavior started at the beginning of 1985, when he'd been with me nearly four years. He became less and less interested in his food. At the same time, he stayed outdoors for much longer intervals, even in bitter winter cold. When he did come back in he'd eat little or nothing — of exactly the same foods he'd been consuming and enjoying ever since he arrived.

Was he freeloading meals elsewhere? Highly unlikely, since his ID tag with my name and phone number was immediately readable to anyone who got close enough to feed him a handout. Nevertheless, I tried an experiment in early February, keeping him confined inside the house for four days in a row. Throughout, he barely picked at each of his two daily meals, never finishing more than half of his normal ration. After that, I had the vet check him over carefully. But no apparent medical explanation could be found for his two odd symptoms: loss of appetite and prolonged absences.

Finally, a glimmer of light. Late one frigid evening I had a phone call from my neighbors Ian and Frank, a few houses away. Would I please drive over there and collect Tim? they begged me; he stubbornly refused to go home on his own. Each time they put him outside and pointed him toward my house, he'd hang around crying to be let back in.

Suddenly the whole situation became clear. Tim had been visiting the two men enough to decide that he really preferred their home to mine.

At that point they were keeping no house pets, though they were fond of cats. Ian still mourned his own cherished longhaired cat who had died a couple of years earlier. Frank sometimes fed neighborhood stray cats outdoors on their deck. Both were delighted whenever Tim came by for a visit and settled in for a cozy snooze by their fireplace. But knowing — and respecting — that he was my pet, not theirs, they fed him nothing more than an occasional treat. And, each time he'd enjoyed their hospitality for a while, they firmly ushered him out to go back to his own home. Yet Tim refused to go. He made clear that he wanted to move in and stay in *their* house, once and for all.

Why? Because he had shown no signs of unhappiness until now, we could only speculate. The most plausible theory: when an opportunity to be an Only Pet presented itself, he voted for the exclusive status and privileges that go with that lifestyle.

Next question: Were Ian and Frank willing to take over complete responsibility for Tim? Obviously I couldn't relinquish my own four-year role as caregiver — attending to his medical checkups and needs, keeping him tagged and identified as my pet with my phone number, regularly serving his meals and all the rest — unless they agreed to a full-fledged, official adoption.

So we had an exchange of correspondence. On March 8 I wrote to Ian and Frank: "I've hardly seen Timbo at all over the past week or so — he comes by now and then but won't come into the house — and imagine he is spending much of his indoor time with you with a view to a permanent new home. Here are a few useful things to know about him...." I then summarized the vaccinations he was due for and his general medical condition. I warned about the flea allergy and the fur matting and outlined his feeding habits and tastes. Moving on to his personality, I wrote:

"I suspect one of the reasons for Tim's rejection of this home (in which nothing new has occurred!) is that he would ideally like to live outdoors at night and sleep indoors all day. This may well be a cat's true nature. But I do not allow it with my cats. The one major concession I ask from them, in exchange for a secure and loving home, is that they stay safely indoors after dark. In practice, this means when they come in for dinner, they stay in until after breakfast the next day. Of course any cat can choose to pass up the evening meal and stay out — and nearly all of mine do that now and then. But Tim would like to do the Night-Hunter-Born-Free bit every night. Or maybe he'd like to be Only Cat in a household. (He's always had at least two other feline siblings here — gets along with them fine.)

"Who knows? Who can read the mind of a cat?.... Let's see what he wants to do with his life! Meanwhile, I think I'd better leave the ID tag with my phone number on his collar for the time being. If you and he mutually decide to form a permanent relationship (or at least for as long as he had one with me), we can talk later about official transfer of ID, medical records, etc.I can't say I really miss him a great deal — the other three cats are delightful and affectionate company — but I'd like to feel assured that you are giving him the shelter, comfort and companionship that he requires. Good luck!"

Six days later, Ian — an artist who worked at home but exhibited his paintings in various galleries — replied graciously and at length:

"Thank you for your kind and generous letter regarding Tim. You are right, he seems to have moved in. I've been somewhat upset and embarrassed by the situation, and my embarrassment has kept me from calling you to keep you informed.

"I'd like to reiterate that I don't think we actively or intentionally attempted to take your cat away from you. In fact, I insisted I didn't want a pet. A couple of years ago I lost my beloved Spotty Cat, and her death caused me so much suffering for so long that I decided 'never again.' Last summer we had to put our old dog to sleep and there was more sorrow. Both Frank and I said no more pets, at least for a long while. Though the house had a tangible emptiness when they were gone, the one positive aspect was a new sense of freedom. I spend a lot of time in New York, and I should spend more for the sake of my career, and then, of course, we go to Florida; and suddenly we had the freedom to lock the door and leave without making arrangements for pets and worrying if they would be alright.

"When Timmy started to come by we would let him in for a short visit and occasionally a snack (I think because he reminded me of Spotty Cat), and I thought I had the best of both worlds because I had a fuzzy creature to visit with for a while without the attachment and responsibility of owning a pet. Frank, in fact, refers to him as our "Part-Time Cat." However, it seems that Timmy had different ideas. He started to stay longer and longer and I began to suspect a takeover. Therefore, I put him out and insisted he stay out — but he wouldn't leave. I've even taken him to the edge of the property, pointed him toward home, and stamped my feet and clapped my hands to chase him away — and in a few minutes he'd be back on the porch.

"We would go to New York and two or three days later come back to find him waiting for us. A few nights ago I put him out at 4:30 PM (I always put him out at this time, thinking he'll go home to eat) and we went to a friend's house for dinner. When we got back at 1:30 in the morning he was waiting for us — so, of course, I let him in and fed him. Timmy first started to stay overnight because I stay up late working or reading and sometimes go to bed at 2 or 3 in the morning and he would be outside reaching for the doorknob or shivering on the doormat. Since I figured you were probably asleep, I couldn't leave him out overnight because I was worried about dogs or the cold.

"Contrary to your description I find him a charming cat and very affectionate. It puzzles me why his personality is different here and why he should prefer strangers when he's obviously had years of good attention and care from you. The only thing I can come up with is that he wants to be the 'only cat' and he suddenly discovered what it was like to be the only cat when I stupidly let him in and he had the run of the house for even short periods. I thought I understood the psychology of cats, but this is a strange situation, and now I don't think I understand even myself to have allowed myself to get this involved.

"I've been upset over the situation, even though we enjoy having Timmy around, because I felt like a thief and that this was not something to do to a neighbor. Your letter has made me feel better, and thank you for being so understanding. I hope there are not too many bad feelings, and please rest assured that as long as Timmy stays with us (he's not locked up and goes in and out all day) he will get the love and attention our former pets received. Thank you for your kind offer of paying for the shots but since he is here we will take care of such matters. Your letter has allowed me to enjoy having him around even more, but I won't think of him as our cat — I think we should wait and see what happens. Very best regards, Ian."

What happened was predictable. No wait was needed for Tim's full-time transition to Ian and Frank's pet. No competition! No restrictions! No need to share territory, attention, toys, water dish, litterbox or anything else with other animals. He was now sole cat, once and future king of his household, free to come and go as he pleased and write his own ticket on anything his new humans were willing to indulge him in. From what I could gather, they spoiled him rotten. (They can't contradict me; both are no longer living now.) If Tim felt an urge to prowl the neighborhood in the middle of the night, they obediently got up to let him out — and back in again when he'd had enough. They took him along to Florida every year, keeping him cool and comfy in their air-conditioned condo.

I saw him only occasionally, when he chose to wander through my back yard (for old times' sake?). One day, two months *after* he had moved out, I took a snapshot of him posed ornamentally next to some red tulips along my house foundation, looking fully at ease and at home. But never again would he set foot in my home — or even let me touch him. If I ever approached or spoke to him, he scampered away.

Timbo lived on contentedly with his new family for eight and a half more years, until he became ill and died in November 1993. He would then have been about 15, a good healthy life span for a cat. So his life story is basically a happy one. The only harm was to my own vanity from his rejection — and that didn't last too long or cut too deep.

I owe two worthwhile lessons to my experience with Tim:

Even after several years of close cohabitation, and countless affectionate moments, you can never presume to "know" how your cat truly feels about the relationship.

And if your pet should decide one day to reject your home — for whatever apparent reason or lack of one — for heaven's sake, don't argue! Just give in as gracefully as you can.

9

Jenny Columba

A Good, Unadventurous Life

After the loss of a pet, when is the right time to fill the vacancy?

I won't use the word "replace." Because every living creature is unique, it can't be replaced with a duplicate — like a battery, for example — when it dies. And I've found that it's only after the *death* of an animal companion that timing the arrival of a new one may be difficult. There's really no problem if the pet is alive and well and has simply moved out of the home to join another. After I banished Casey, for example, I was ready to welcome his successor as soon as a good candidate became available. Nor did I hesitate after Tim's voluntary self-banishment, or the departure of a few later cats who, for one good reason or another, couldn't continue living with me.

But when a loved pet is deceased, the bereaved owner may find the idea of taking in a new animal disloyal and distressing. Some owners can't face it at all. I've known animal lovers, as perhaps you have, who swear "never again!" after suffering the death of a cherished dog or cat. (I'm afraid I can't sympathize! To my mind they're being unpardonably selfish — focused on their own feelings at the expense of some poor lonely animal that desperately needs a home in order to survive.) But there are no rules or norms, of course. When, if ever, to bring in a successor is a highly individual decision, for each family in each case. Ideally we should always be free to wait, under no pressure, until the time feels comfortably right to introduce a new pet.

In my own case I've usually chosen to wait several months after a bereavement before seeking another cat. I need time to adjust to my departed pet's absence, to honor its memory with a respectful period of mourning. No less important, the surviving pets in my multi-cat household also need time to get used to the situation. At least I think they do! Cats may mope less visibly than dogs when unhappy. But they are certainly aware of the sudden disappearance of a long-familiar sibling — and the arrival of a stranger to take its place. Some adapt to the change more easily than others.

Once, I was left with two adoptive brothers who had spent more than a decade together with their just-deceased sister. Both had medical problems. So this time I decided not to fill the void at all. Instead, I'd let my elderly little gents live out the rest of their lives in undisturbed peace, as a twosome. Unfortunately, a few months later a rescue crisis arose and we found ourselves saddled with a third male cat (see Chico's story)

On two occasions, though, I made an exception to my general rule. Immediately after a pet died, I rushed out to acquire another as soon as possible. The first time, Jenny was the new cat I brought home.

Lucy's death in October 1981 was a devastating blow — as I probably made clear when I told you about it. I was stunned and bewildered by grief. True, she hadn't left me alone; I still had the company of Rosalie (for a few more months) and Tim (for three more years). But the emptiness with my Lucy gone — just the sight of her unused food dish at breakfast that first morning — was hard to bear. I felt an urgent need for some new activity, a keep-busy responsibility to distract me from brooding over my loss.

So a few hours after I placed her in her grave, I paid a visit to a kennel where my humane group boarded some of their adoptable dogs and cats. There, I was drawn to a little orange-and-white tabby kitten, barely four months old. A few weeks earlier she had been dumped, together with her black-and-white brother, at the side of a busy highway. They were rescued in the dead of night by a volunteer who worked with our group. Her littermate had already been adopted. She was friendly and sweet, so I just scooped her up and took her home with me. I left a note telling the humane office that she would now be my foster pet, pending official adoption if she fit in with my other resident cats.

As I hoped, they were compatible. The presence of this very young, gentle little creature posed no challenge to Rosalie or Tim and both accepted her easily. For my part, to help take my mind off Lucy, it was a relief to have a new animal making demands on my attention, needing to be fussed over and familiarized with

the household. It would take me a while to form a close attachment to Jenny, but I appreciated her from the start.

I named her after the red-headed heroines of *The Threepenny
Opera* and other Kurt Weill musicals. "Columba" was added because — unforgettably! — she joined our home on Columbus
Day. She stayed for the next 12 years, minus a month. If I sort my
long-term felines into chronological groups, Jenny was the first
member of my Second Generation.

Of her cat contemporaries, Jenny had "the cutest face, the softest fur, the loudest purr" — as I ticked off her superlatives for
outsiders. While not prone to baby talk, I called her "my cutie-
pie" so often that the endearment ended up inscribed on her
gravestone; my other nickname for her was "Jennikin." She was
easygoing, not too demanding, timid though not fearful, reserved
with strangers but warmly affectionate with me — a classic lap
cat who loved to have her tummy rubbed. She was also bright and
resourceful, a gluttonous eater, an adept though infrequent
hunter.

Jenny bonded quickly with the other cats, perhaps because
she'd been socialized from the start with her littermate(s). But
her great love was Toby. You'll hear about him in the next chapter; he arrived nearly six months after she did. Did he fill a role
left vacant by the little black-and-white brother with whom she'd
been abandoned on the highway? Whatever Toby represented for
her, she adored him immediately and they became inseparable.
In practice, *she* was the one who attached herself to *him*. It was
always Jenny who jumped up to join Toby on his chair, always she
who initiated the tumbling, wrestling or reciprocal washing. But
he responded with equal gusto. My snapshot collection has many
gems of the two Little Lovers ecstatically embracing or energeti-
cally grooming each other — or just dozing peacefully entwined.

Occasionally, I'd be awakened during the night by churning movements on my blanket: Jenny and Toby would be engaged in a mutual love-and-laundering fest, clutching each other as their tongues massaged furiously. Every now and then Jenny (who was spayed, of course) would be carried away by some perverse sexual urge to the point of mounting Toby (who was neutered, of course). Toby did *not* care for this overture and his emphatic protest would bring that particular session to an end.

To my regret, I've never had any other pets who enjoyed grooming each other as Jenny and Toby did. I envy the owners luckier than I with their cats; their mutual washing is such a delightful and endearing ritual to watch. One later pet of mine, Freddy, would occasionally lick the head of one of his sisters. She'd put up with it for a couple of minutes and then hiss at him to get lost — fearing (correctly) that his tender touch would soon intensify to some rougher play wrestling.

While Toby was her special soul mate, Jenny got along with all the other cats who shared her home — and who (after Rosalie died when Jenny was still a kitten) *all happened to be male* –– until Cindy moved in in September 1992. I'll save the details of their incompatibility for Cindy's own chapter. Here, I'll just note how bitterly Jenny resented the first female (a fully adult female, at that) to encroach on her turf in the nearly 11 years she had reigned, unchallenged, as queen. Maybe it was something other than the newcomer's gender that so antagonized Jenny; no way to know for sure. She didn't physically attack Cindy. But she harassed and intimidated the poor creature into a state of fearful misery. Their cold war made me pretty miserable too. If the two couldn't manage to coexist peacefully, and one cat had to go, then of course the long-resident Jenny would stay. She deserved my first loyalty and her well-being took priority.

Jenny's life was, on the whole, pleasantly uneventful. She was a prudent puss. I can't recall a single instance of her getting into trouble. She took ample advantage of her outdoor privileges and enjoyed cruising the immediate neighborhood, chasing small rodents around our yard and the adjoining woods and hedgerow. But she never stayed out late. She never ventured to cross the street, with its murderous traffic. She never attacked, or was attacked by, a hostile animal large enough to do her harm (dog, feral cat, raccoon, fox, pheasant, whatever). She never climbed a tree that she couldn't easily get down from.

One spring day, before she was a year old, she worked her way up through a large arborvitae next to the house and leaped onto the roof. There she paced back and forth in confusion, wailing plaintively. I had enough time to take a snapshot of her silhouetted prettily against the sky. Before too long, with my entreaties from below, she summoned the nerve to jump back into the dense evergreen and work her way down.

Only one serious mishap befell her. In August 1983 I was away most of the month traveling in Siberia and Central Asia. My live-in cat sitter for this lengthy absence was my cousin Jan, accompanied by her young son and her dog. Muffin was a medium-sized, mixed-breed shelter dog. She was well-behaved and friendly to one and all, including cats. I have a photo of her playing with one of my four felines then in residence. But it wasn't Jenny; she, sad to say, was badly spooked by this alien animal. The first time she was let outdoors after Muffin arrived, she ran off — and never came back the entire time I was gone.

Driving home from the airport, Jan told me that Jenny hadn't approached the house once for a meal or anything else during my three-and-a-half-week absence. But she was alive and nearby; every now and then Jan could glimpse her little face peering out from the shrubbery in the hedgerow. As soon as we reached home I raced into the backyard and began calling Jenny. She emerged from the brush almost immediately and came to me.

She looked semi-starved. Contrary to what many people think, house cats accustomed to a diet of nutritious, balanced commercial pet food are *not* able to replace this — automatically or adequately — simply by hunting mice and other wild prey. Jenny may have caught an occasional rodent or bird to subsist on. She must have slaked her thirst from puddles of rainwater. But she was so painfully thin, with her ID collar hanging so loosely, that one of her front legs had become hooked through it and immobilized.

Cradling Jenny securely in my arms, I shouted across the yard to Jan: Please take Muffin *away from the house right now*! And don't bring her back for at least a half-hour! Once they were gone, I brought Jenny indoors, carefully cut the embedded collar free from her neck and armpit (both rubbed raw), and fed her an initial restorative serving of cat food. At the first opportunity I had her checked over by the vet. Luckily, she had no infected wounds or other lasting ill effects from her ordeal. I kept her quietly inside the house for a good while and she soon gained back the weight she'd lost.

Her misadventure was no one's fault, of course. Jenny's lonely, hungry outdoor exile for nearly a month was entirely her own initiative. In effect she punished herself, voluntarily and quite harshly, for her timidity toward a sweet-natured, inoffensive dog that her three feline siblings were willing to make friends with. (Some nine years afterwards, another cat you'll hear about later also ran off to a neurotically self-imposed exile. That time, the outcome was much grimmer.) It was Jenny's worst experience and she was fortunate to come through it so well.

It was at any rate her worst *non-medical* experience. Through-out her agreeable, fairly long and relatively uneventful life, Jenny's most difficult time came toward its end — and was entirely due to ill health. I'll spare you some of the blow-by-blow. But the progression of her illness provided me with a vital part of my education in living with cats — notably as they grow older.

Just as humans who live long enough to become senior citizens develop more complex (and costly!) health problems, so do our longer-lived pets. Lucy and Rosalie had both been cruelly torn from me at the mid-point of a cat's normal 15-year life span. Casey, still a child, had been given away early to re-start his life. Tim, approaching *his* midlife, chose of his own volition to dump me and recycle himself elsewhere. So Jenny, the fifth cat to enter this stage of my life, was the first to remain with me until her senior years.

Before she reached age 11 she hadn't needed any veterinary care beyond routine maintenance: an annual checkup and regular vaccinations against distemper, rabies and feline leukemia. Then, in midsummer 1992, she suddenly began vomiting during the night, every night for about five days, plus some diarrhea. The vet, having examined her and found no fever or swelling, hypothesized that her symptoms were caused by a ball of fur lodged in the digestive tract that she couldn't manage to spit up. Laxatone, a lubricant-laxative for dissolving hairballs, was administered for a week or so and Jenny responded well. Then, she immediately came down with a respiratory infection and needed antibiotic treatment for another 10 days. By mid-August, thankfully, she was fine again. But this, her first bout with any illness, was only a minor prologue to her major trouble ahead.

Six months later, in February 1993, she again started vomiting. This time, the hairball remedy didn't help. Nor did a couple of other treatments that the doctor at my local animal hospital suggested trying. Eventually, he referred me to a veterinary gastroenterologist, some 50 miles away.

The specialist examinined Jenny, her X-rays, and the laboratory report on her complete blood profile. He first thought she could be afflicted with simple gastritis (inflammation of the stomach). Before subjecting her to an invasive endoscopy, he prescribed a therapeutic trial with Tagamet, an antacid medication often used to treat ulcers. Unfortunately, this was of no help. So, two weeks later, I drove Jenny back to the gastroenterologist to be admitted for an endoscopy. This surgical procedure, performed under anesthesia, inserts equipment to survey and biopsy the stomach.

The result was bad news: cancer. The medical terminology, "infiltrating lymphosarcoma" or "gastric neoplasia," means a malignant stomach tumor. It is fairly common in cats, the specialist told me. I now had three options: One, euthanasia. Second, treatment with Prednisone (cortisone). This anti-inflammatory steroid, he said, could be "somewhat therapeutic" and even achieve a short-term remission, but wasn't likely to be helpful in the long term. Third, since surgery isn't practicable for this kind of cancer, my remaining option was chemotherapy. Needless to say, I considered this my *only* option.

The specialist warned me that the chemo protocol involved some very costly drugs and "the prognosis must remain guarded." On the hopeful side, her tumor was in an early clinical stage with no involvement of the lymph nodes. We arranged that he'd set up the schedule of injections and my primary veterinarian would then order the drugs he prescribed to be administered to Jenny at our local hospital. Throughout the chemotherapy I would also have to give her Prednisone pills orally, twice a day, at home.

Jenny's treatments began at the end of April. The next four months were arduous. Observing her closely, maintaining a daily record of her condition and food intake, medicating her, transporting her to and from the hospital for her chemo injections (two 25-mile round trips each time), encouraging her to eat, worrying about her failing appetite and growing weakness…. It made for a stressful summer. Yet I still had my Jennikin with me. There was still hope.

Then, in early August, she virtually lost interest in food. Her weight declined alarmingly. Another blood-chemistry profile, a week's inpatient care at the gastroenterologist's hospital, and finally a second endoscopy, yielded a bitter verdict. Jenny's stomach cancer seemed to be in remission, but now her *kidneys* had failed. She was suffering from what is called Chronic Renal Disease. Although the specialist tried her on one or two new therapeutic products, he wrote me: "I think the prognosis is guarded to poor…but we will try our best to help her for as long as possible."

My gut feeling was that the end was near. Did I want to watch Jenny starve to death day by day? Just after Labor Day I dug a grave for her. I sent a note to my local veterinarian's associate, a deft and compassionate young doctor named Carol who had been administering Jenny's chemotherapy treatments:

"She is failing quite fast. Eats virtually nothing unless force-fed. Lethargic, wobbly on her feet, getting thinner and thinner. It is pathetic to watch her and keep jamming medications into her that are doing her no visible good. I think the Time of Decision is quite near. I don't want Jenny to deteriorate into a zombie before she dies."

I asked Carol to make an exception to the hospital's normal policy and come to the house to perform euthanasia: "Jenny has been through so much physical and emotional trauma that I want the end to be the least upsetting possible, preferably in her own home. I can guarantee that she would not hide, struggle or resist handling. You yourself have seen how pliable and gentle she is, and of course she is now quite used to being handled by you."

After one or two last-ditch medication efforts, a home visit appointment was set. It was a beautiful mid-September day. When Carol arrived, with a veterinary technician to assist her, Jenny was dozing on an upper shelf in the guest-room closet. I had never known her to set foot there before in all the years she lived with me — but this was consistent with the tendency of cats to want to hide when they are dying. At my request, Carol took a goodbye photo of Jenny in my arms; the garden in which she'd spent so many pleasant hours was visible in the background. Then, on the same kitchen counter where I'd been regularly medicating her, she was given her final injection. It was so quick and merciful; one tiny throb, and she was gone.

The doctor's helper placed Jenny in her shroud — again one of my own pillowcases, now a tradition launched by Lucy. After they left I cried a little and ate some lunch. Then I buried my girl, with three freshly cut roses (Brandy, Mister Lincoln and Peace, according to my notes) placed atop the shroud before the grave was filled in. A few weeks later I planted a trio of orange-cupped daffodils at the foot of the stone, to bloom next spring.

Jenny was my first pet to be euthanized. The decision to have it done at home is one I can recommend to other pet owners without reservation — provided, of course, that the circumstances make it practical. Obviously, any pet already hospitalized is more comfortably and conveniently put to sleep right there. My only other experience, at this writing, was with a cat being treated in a specialized hospital far from home. After learning the specialist's dismal prognosis I authorized the procedure over the phone. But — I hope you agree — a pet spending its final days in the familiar surroundings of its own home is so much better off, under so much less emotional stress, if a veterinarian is able to pay a house call for the euthanasia. Not to mention how much less stressful it is for a sorrowing owner to be spared the ordeal of transporting a terminally ill pet to the execution chamber.

Let me include here a comment on costs. My records show that in 1993, the year of Jenny's terminal illness, I spent $3,264 on her *non-routine* medical care. Even so, her expenses accounted for only two-thirds of my total veterinary outlay. Because my other two cats at the time had their own medical problems, 1993 was an exceptionally expensive year.

I don't begrudge one penny of whatever I must spend to provide my pets with the best available health care. But I'm not wealthy. And, after weighing the pros and cons of veterinary insurance, I haven't found this to be worthwhile for someone in my situation. So all those extra pennies for my pets' non-routine medical needs just have to come out of pocket — no tax deductions, no discounts, no reimbursements. Moreover, the longer they are lucky enough to live, the more likely their medical needs will expand. This is a costly reality all animal lovers need to be aware of, and have no illusions about, whenever we take on the responsibility for an animal's lifetime care.

Jenny had a *good* lifetime. It lasted as long as any quality survived. I loved and enjoyed her and am happy for both of us that I spent as much as it took to make her last months as livable as possible. The gloom of losing her battle with disease had one silver lining. At least she pre-deceased Toby! If her adored brother had died before her, she would have been inconsolable.

10

Toby

The Best Cat

His superlative, chosen with care to inscribe on his gravestone, was easily earned.

It wasn't that I *loved* Toby most of all my cats. (I think that distinction will always belong to Lucy.) But I *valued* him most. To this day! His sterling qualities, which visitors to our home appreciated as much as I did, made him the closest thing to a perfect pet I've ever lived with.

He was unpretentiously handsome: basically mouse-gray, with tabby stripes that faded as he grew older , and off-white highlights extending from his mouth down through his underside. Neat round little head, yellow eyes, compact build. Bright, quick, playful, resourceful, a superb hunter. He was unselfish and undemanding, a noncompetitive friend to all his fellow cats, and warmly responsive to Jenny's huge affection for him. Besides my so-called X-rated photos of the Little Lovers in unbridled passion, I have snapshots of Toby snuggled happily on a sofa together with two or three feline companions.

He had a sweet nature, a dignified demeanor, beautiful manners. Unique among all my cats, he played gracious host to my guests like any well-brought-up young gentleman of the house. At dinner parties he'd tour the room to greet each friend in turn, adding a brief lap visit if the guest cared to pet him. "He was the dearest, smartest ," wrote one frequent visitor in condolence, "and I knew that the first time I ever met him and saw no reason to change my mind over the years.... He was just so *nice* and welcoming. He is a major loss."

I had my fond, unimaginative epithets for him: Neat and sweet. Ept, kempt and couth. My little gray guy. My Tobie-cat.... So far he enjoys the status of my longest-lived cat, having spent with me more than 12 of his total 14 or 15 years. Those years, unlike Jenny's, were eventful. He had ample adventures and mishaps even without the health problems of his later years. If the adage about cats having nine lives holds true, Toby used up a substantial number of his.

Like so many free-roaming cats wearing no identification, his origins are unknown. Veterinarians estimated he'd been born no later than early 1980, perhaps the year before. When he first turned up homeless in January 1981, in the yard of two men who maintained a second home in the country, he was still young but full-grown, already neutered, easy to approach and friendly. All of which suggested that he'd been someone's house pet. What drove him from his home in the middle of winter? Was he accidentally lost or deliberately abandoned? Why had he become a stray? There were no obvious clues then — though a startling one, which I'm saving to tell later, came to light many years afterward.

His finders, Mark and Richard, asked around their neighborhood for his possible owner but found no one missing a pet cat. So they began looking after him. They fed him and gave him a warm place to sleep whenever they were in the country house; when they were away in the city, neighbors pitched in to help. They called him "Paddy," appreciated that he got along with their dog, even took him for a brief stay in their city apartment.

But after a full year, in January 1982, Mark and Richard closed up their house and moved away for good. "Paddy" was left at the mercy of kind-hearted neighbors, especially one named Lillian. The winter was bitter cold. Lillian wasn't able to keep the cat as an indoor pet (I forget why) and the nights were too icy to leave him outside. So she brought him to the humane group from which I had adopted Tim and Jenny. They, in turn, boarded him at the same kennel where I had found Jenny a few months earlier, on Columbus Day.

At this point — to clarify the time line — I had three cats at home: Rosalie, Tim and little newly-adopted Jenny. But then, in early February, came Rosalie's fatal accident. I spent much of March traveling, leaving my two remaining pets in the care of a live-in sitter. At the beginning of April, soon after returning home, I paid an exploratory visit to the boarding kennel. I wasn't in any great hurry to acquire a new cat. And I felt that when I did, a female would probably be the best choice; less competition for Tim.

But — there sat Toby, neat and sweet in his cage. He appealed to me instantly. So that was that!

≈

Here, let me digress for a bit to talk about pet sitters. I hope you agree that they are virtually indispensable to all of us who keep cats and have occasion to be away from home without taking them along.

What about boarding our pets? This suits many dogs splendidly; several of my dog-owning friends swear by it. But for cats, boarding is never a desirable option. Most hate to be moved out of their family homes and don't adjust easily to any change of scene. They're upset by strange surroundings, noises and odors, unfamiliar people and animals. So boarding is best reserved for unforeseen emergencies *only* — and then never in a commercial kennel where dogs predominate. Once or twice I've been obliged to board my cats, at their veterinarian's, when I had to be hospitalized on short notice with no time to arrange for a pet sitter. But normally I make advance plans for one *every* time I expect to be absent from home overnight or longer.

Over the years I've developed a pretty reliable system. It may not correspond to your own preferences for cat care while you're away. But it's worked well for me and mine. So, in case it can give you any useful ideas, I'll summarize my arrangements.

I use what I call a *walk-in* sitter for short absences from home: one, two, at most three nights. The sitter visits the house twice a day to feed and water the cats, pet and play with them for a while, attend to the litter boxes, check that everything is in good order. In the warm months she has my permission to let the cats outdoors during daylight hours, if they wish. Otherwise they remain inside the house.

My walk-in sitter is given a typed list of whatever I expect her to do and that she might need to know. This includes feeding instructions, safety precautions, veterinarian's name and number, special notes on the animals' behavior. I also try to leave a phone number where I can be reached in emergency.

Animal lovers who work as walk-in sitters aren't hard to find. They leave their business cards at veterinary hospitals and pet-supply stores; many advertise in local papers. A few consider it their principal work and may even belong to the National Association of Professional Pet Sitters. They should always be ready to supply references, easily checked, from their pet-owning clients in the community.

Visiting pet sitters' fees are generally not negotiable. The amounts vary depending on how many dogs and/or cats are involved, the number of daily visits, the need for medication, grooming or other special care. A pet owner deterred by the cost can always try to work out an arrangement with a friend, neighbor or relative in which no money changes hands — perhaps reciprocal pet care with another owner who travels from time to time. I myself have never found a good opportunity to do this. But I prefer, in any case, a straightforward business arrangement to reliance on favors from people I might feel morally indebted to.

It's a different situation when I plan to be away more than two or three days. Then, I arrange for a *live-in* sitter. I just don't feel comfortable leaving my pets to spend long hours alone for days and nights on end, their solitude relieved only by brief caretaker visits. So I look for someone who will sleep in the house and spend most evenings there, even if my cats have to be left on their own during the sitter's daytime working hours. The ideal candidate — not always available! — is a person "in-and-out" throughout the day: perhaps working part-time, doing self-employed work from home, retired, or on vacation.

What does this cost? For me, it depends on the time of year. I happen to live in a popular resort area. So I've been lucky to have rarely had to pay for a resident sitter when I travel during the summer season. Out-of-town friends or relatives (like my cousin Jan), or warmly recommended friends of friends, have usually been available to move in and take tender loving care of my cats in exchange for a rent-free beach holiday. For my part, I'm usually glad to escape the frenetic summer scene for a while — and get back home in time for my own favorite season, fall. Everyone benefits!

But at other times of year I can rarely count on vacationing friends to look after my cats. Ideally, I like to get away for two or three weeks in the dead of winter. I've also signed on for an occasional tempting trip in late fall or early spring. (As you may have guessed, travel is my favorite treat.) On those occasions I need to employ a local resident willing to move into my house for the duration.

How to find someone? Pet sitters qualified and willing to live in — "do overnights," they call it — never advertise this availability. Why would they? They'd hardly have any time left to spend in their own homes! Their reputations become known strictly by word of mouth. By asking around, you might hear of someone endorsed by pet-owning friends or the staff at your veterinarian's office. But such research can take time. And even a highly recommended candidate might turn out to be *already* booked for another pet-sitting job on the very dates you'll be away. This has happened to me more than once.

Solution? *I'm* the one who does the advertising! Several times over the years I've placed a classified ad under "Pets" in a couple of my community's weeklies, at least two months before my planned trip. The ad usually reads: "LIVE-IN CAT SITTER needed from [month/day] to [month/day]. Must be mature, responsible, experienced caring for cats. References essential. [My phone number]."

It works! At least a dozen people always respond. I'm ready with a barrage of questions to fire over the phone: How much experience have you had staying with other people's cats? Your age? (I won't engage anyone under 25.) If you have pets of your own, who will take care of them while you're living in someone else's home? How many hours each day will you normally be away from the house at work? Phone numbers of at least two references, please. Then — if everything else sounds satisfactory — what daily fee do you charge?

The phone vetting streamlines my applicant list fast. Each time it produces one *best* candidate. After I've checked her references — all but one of my hired sitters have been women — we set up a short introductory meeting. In addition, I keep on file the names of two or three other qualified respondents as backup. This is in case of last-minute illness or family emergency with my first choice, and for potential future contact.

I've also saved names on a blacklist of people to *avoid* employing at any time. These include the 18- and 19-year-olds (how do they understand the word "mature" in the ad?); the people who'd have no scruples about leaving their own pets unattended at home ("I'll stop in to check on them now and then"); and the people greedy enough to announce at the outset how much they expect to be paid (this should properly be the *last* item on the agenda).

For the sitters I've chosen to hire, as well as for the friends who will be assuming the same responsibilities for free in summer, I prepare two detailed documents. One covers house-sitting, the other cat care. The basic information is stored on my computer and easily updated for each of my absences. Together, they add up to a snow job, far more data than the sitters want to read or — most of the time — will need to know in practice. But I feel more secure if every possible contingency has been touched on. (Where to call for a plumber? Is there a second cat carrier in case *two* pets urgently need transport to the vet? If the resident sitter is suddenly called away in emergency, who can provide walk-in cat care on short notice?)

Wrapping up my three cardinal rules: First, *plan and book a sitter well in advance*. (Usually I start recruiting as soon as I've confirmed my reservation for a trip — even a trip months away.) Second, *scrupulously check all references* of anyone not already well known. Third, *insist the sitter take time to review the written instructions*, preferably by mailing them to her well before the departure date, so any questions can be cleared up in good time.

A lot of time and effort? Right! But the reward is peace of mind. Freed of worries about my cats' safety and well-being, I've been able to relax and enjoy my travels thousands of miles from home. Best of all, once a new sitter has been tried and served well, arrangements for future absences become that much easier and faster.

After three decades of relying on sitters, I can state flatly that my pets have never had a bad experience. True, one young woman I hired neglected to water my house plants. Another must have been looking after someone's dog in my basement, because weeks later I discovered some dried dung on its floor. A third forgot (I presume) that she had left a pornographic tape in my video cassette recorder.

But none of this had the slightest effect on my cats! I always came home to find them happy and perfectly well cared for.

Now let's get back to Toby's arrival.

He fit in immediately and beautifully. I have snapshots of him the first month he joined the family relaxing near his new siblings, Tim and Jenny, and already enfolded in a grooming embrace with Jenny. In later years, as new cats arrived to live in his home, he accepted them without resentment. From an animal behaviorist's perspective, this suggests that Toby had started life in a litter of contented and playful kittens, happily secure, easy friends to each other and all the people and pets who surrounded them. My caption on one of Toby's chummy group photos reads: "Everybody's littermate!"

Some five and a half years of trouble-free living elapsed before Toby's first real mishap. Late in October 1987 I returned from a trip to learn from my worried sitter that my little gray guy hadn't come home at all the night before. The next day I discovered him sitting next to the house, silent and immobile, with a nasty open wound on his thigh. In the opinion of the vet who stitched him up, the gash might have been made by barbed wire. Had he gouged himself trying to escape from a nearby horse pasture? I'd never know.

His next serious wound, three years later, was badly abscessed and appeared to have been inflicted in a fight. Had he had a violent run-in with a raccoon or feral cat, even a fox or large owl? This would certainly have occurred after dark, on one of the evenings he chose to ignore my dinner call and stay out for a few extra hours of nocturnal adventure.

Toby was by no means my only cat with this unnerving misbehavior. (The first was Rosalie.) I can't count the times I've arrived home from a late evening out to find a wayward puss transfixed in my headlights — or waiting impatiently by the door for the belated meal he (or she) had been summoned to hours earlier. Every time I scolded my naughty pet for having caused me worry. And every time — well, almost every time — I was too relieved by his (or her) safe return to withhold the food as punishment.

But in Toby's case, staying out late was his *only* fault. Otherwise, his behavior was unfailingly considerate and proper. Without this one flaw he would have been too good to be true — a saint! Which brings to mind a strange episode that I committed to paper when it happened. To this day, I don't understand his motivation:

On a mid-September evening in 1990 Toby arrived home just a little late for dinner — and then, when the door was opened for him, *refused* to come inside. He spent the entire night out in the rain. Next morning he reappeared outside the door — but again declined to come in! Not a sign of him all day. That evening, having skipped two meals over the past 24 hours, he turned up promptly at dinnertime, trotted in eagerly, and devoured every morsel in his dish. I left him strictly alone. I was waiting for some kind of apology from him for having rudely snubbed his home *and* his mom!

I finished my own dinner and was typing up my note on his odd behavior. Suddenly Toby jumped on the desk and began to nuzzle me, insistently. We had a *great* love-in. All was well! Without words, he reassured me that after nearly eight and a half years together he hadn't rejected me. But the question still nagged: what had his problem been? One theory is that he had been mesmerized by the sounds and scents of nocturnal prey as the fall harvest and hunting season got under way. Another possibility: a temporary loss of appetite from indigestion held him at a distance from food. Then, after he'd regained his normal hunger and downed a hearty meal, he felt happy enough for an orgy of affection.

Whatever caused this episode, it was the only one of its kind. But it was one of the innumerable times I've wished with all my heart — as I'm sure you have too: *if only we and our pets could explain things to each other!*

By the time Toby had passed his (estimated) 11th birthday, and had been with me a little more than nine years, his medical troubles began in earnest. From summer 1991 until his end three years later, he was a frequent patient at the veterinarary hospital. Don't worry, I won't burden you with a chronological blow-by-blow. For me, it's been not only tedious but painful to review the thick store of health records filed in Toby's memorial album. But I do want to recap his multiple problems for you. They illustrate the vulnerabilities to which so many of our older cats are prone as well as my own speedy (if unsought) education in feline health care.

Twice, a couple of years apart, Toby was afflicted by Lyme disease, a debilitating bacterial infection transmitted by the bite of a deer tick (*Ixodes scapularis*). These little buggers are widespread throughout much of the Northeast and overabundant in the county where I live. Veterinarians are more accustomed to treating dogs for Lyme disease; they consider cats much less susceptible to illness from tick bites. But my own vet happened to be an inspired diagnostician. He recognized and guessed the right reason for Toby's symptoms — even though they differed in each of the two attacks. The first time, he was totally lethargic. The second time he appeared "arthritic," limping on one leg with stiffness in his shoulder and back. Both times the treatment was identical — three weeks of antibiotic tablets — and fully successful.

Ironically, this was only a few years before the appearance on the market of a highly effective insecticide product, named Frontline, for killing ticks as well as fleas on dogs and cats. Nowadays, since all my indoor-outdoor cats are scrupulously protected throughout the tick season with Frontline treatment, I have few worries about a reappearance of Lyme disease among my pets. (I have, however, come down with it myself. Alas, no version of Frontline for humans has been developed yet. All we can do is smear ourselves with repellents and pluck off any ticks we find.)

Toby's next — and major — ailment was hyperthyroidism. This is a common affliction of senior cats and the veterinary profession has an array of methods to deal with it. Toby started with a medication called Tapazole to lower the excessive production of hormone by his thyroid gland. But this didn't help enough, so the gland was removed surgically in two stages, 14 months apart. After that, he was put on a thyroid replacement hormone called Soloxine for the rest of his days, during which he functioned normally. In addition to medication and surgery, there is a third recommended treatment for hyperthyroidism: radioactive iodine. I don't know if this option was available to Toby at that time and in our area, because it was never proposed by his veterinarian.

About a month after Toby's first thyroid operation, he was hit by a car. One of his favorite neighborhood hangouts was a day-care center across the street near our home. He was in the road heading there one day, oblivious to traffic, when he was struck — but the motorist saw him in time enough to brake and avoid killing him. She considerately stopped, rang my doorbell, told me that she'd seen him run away from the collision toward the day-care center. I went over there, looking around and calling for him. No sign! I asked a teacher to phone my number if any of the staff or children ever spotted my cat.

Three days later Toby was still missing. Late that afternoon, when the day-care premises were silent and deserted, I put on my shabbiest work clothes, tied a scarf around my head, and crawled on my stomach into the dirt and débris *under* the building, shining a flashlight back and forth, calling repeatedly for Toby. Soon, I sensed a faint cry from the far end of the crawl space. There! The flashlight found his little face! Slowly, to my murmurs of encouragement, he hobbled his way toward me. We reunited in a gingerly hug; then he rode home in the carrier I'd brought. One hind leg looked fractured, and he eagerly accepted a meal and a drink, but nothing else seemed to be amiss.

Promptly next day Toby was admitted to the animal hospital. He had never been X-rayed before. When the vet phoned to report on the broken leg he added a question that stunned me: how long ago had Toby been shot? The film clearly showed a bullet lodged near his spine. Naturally I had no idea when and how it arrived there — but it offered a clue to the mystery of his background.

Here's one plausible scenario: Let's suppose that one day, near his first home as a family pet, Toby was out exploring a field or hedgerow. A small gray cat can easily be confused with a rabbit from even a short distance away. A hunter, spotting his shape and color moving through the brush, took a pot shot at him. If he'd been wounded badly enough to collapse, the gunman might have come to pick him up, even taken him to be treated. More likely, he was able to run away and hide. Later he fled further — but was never able to find his way back to his own home. By the time he turned up in Mark and Richard's yard, just after Christmas, his gunshot wound might have healed enough not to be conspicuous.

Whether or not this explains how Toby became a stray a dozen years earlier, his doctor assured me that the long-embedded bullet was doing him no harm; there was no reason to risk trying to extract it now. But his injured leg, unfortunately, failed to mend by itself and he had to undergo surgery to repair the fracture. Given his advancing age and weakened condition from thyroid disease, he wasn't able to walk normally for months.

In October 1993, a year after the car hit him, Toby came home with several puncture wounds on his face close to his right eye. The eye became badly infected. An extended series of treatments followed, including visits to a veterinary ophthalmologist a considerable distance from where we live. His eye problems continued right into the following spring — at which time he began to lose his appetite.

My poor little gray guy was failing. Would I soon be nursing a chronic invalid?

I took Toby for tests to the gastroenterologist who had treated Jenny's cancer. (What with the ophthalmologist and his primary veterinarian, he was now under the simultaneous care of *three* doctors.) No clinical evidence emerged of tumors or abnormalities in the kidneys, liver or pancreas. Antibiotic and anti-inflammatory medication did help him.

By summer 1994 Toby had regained some weight and his ailing eye had stabilized — but now his hearing had begun to go! This was made vividly clear one evening when I summoned the cats in for dinner. I could see Toby a stone's throw from the kitchen, comfortably dozing as he nestled under a hemlock hedge. He failed to respond to my usual whistle. Only when I clapped and called out his name loud and clear did he lift his head, rouse himself and come ambling in.

Finally came a foggy Friday late in August.

I arrived home from an afternoon's errands to find a message on my answering machine from a woman named Deirdre. Driving past my house around three hours earlier, she had come upon the body of my cat in the road. She removed his collar to read his ID tag and note down my phone number. Then, she moved him to the side of the road and covered him with a sheet she happened to have in her car. She expressed her sorrow for my loss.

Later, I'll have quite a bit to say about the importance of equipping cats with legible identification. Now, I'll only stress how deeply grateful I was that Toby didn't end his days as anonymous roadkill, inexplicably missing forever from his family home — and how fortunate I was that a Good Samaritan as compassionate as Deirdre had happened by.

Toby must have died instantly, where he fell; his battered head attested to a merciful quick kill. He was at a point in the road close to the day-care center and had obviously been en route there. Also obvious — to me, at least — was that his failing hearing had deafened him to the noise of approaching traffic. Perhaps, in retrospect, it had also been partly to blame for his first auto accident a couple of years earlier.

I buried Toby immediately. The late-summer daylight lasted long enough to dig a deep, neat grave next to Jenny's under a large Eastern red cedar. I wept a bit as I worked but was thankful for two things: Toby was lucky not to have suffered at the end. Don't we all want to exit as quickly as he did? And though I'd miss him greatly, I was relieved that he wouldn't have to endure losing more of the *quality* in his life as he became more aged and frail. He had, after all, enjoyed around 15 years of a good, comfortable indoor-outdoor life — best of both worlds! — in a devoted family. I, too, was lucky to have been favored so long with his excellent company. No other pet has lived with me as many years.

Toby's departure rang down the curtain on my Second Generation of cats. He was the last to go. Jenny, already gone nearly a year, had been its other leading star. Tim, having rudely resigned, couldn't qualify as a full member of that company. The two other cats who did both joined the family *after* Toby and left *before* him. Now, it's time to meet Harry.

· 11 ·

Harry

A Pet in Need of Pampering

Every cat is special, of course. But three distinctions made Harry a bit more special than others.

He was the sole pet I ever raised from infancy. His health problems were by far the most challenging and complex I've ever had to cope with. And, probably for both these reasons, I think of him as the *neediest* of all my cats — emotionally as well as physically. He depended on my pampering. And I, in turn, became dependent on his need for me.

I certainly didn't choose to foster a newborn. (My admiration for people who do, however, is boundless.) Back in April 1983, the humane group I volunteered with — from which I'd already adopted Tim, Jenny and Toby — was still two years away from opening its own dog and cat shelter. It was then operating out of a cubicle office in the thrift shop it rented, while boarding its adoptable animals in various commercial kennels.

One afternoon a teenager walked into the office to hand over a tiny orphaned kitten — at most ten days old. The infant couldn't be left at a local veterinary hospital; none had staff available to administer round-the-clock feedings. Nor, among the cats then awaiting adoption, did there happen to be any nursing mothers who could add this new kitten to their litter. So it could only survive if hand-raised privately by a human foster parent — starting *now*. Because I'd just happened to stop by the office for some paperwork, I found myself abruptly elected to take the kitten home with me — for that night, at least.

An office assistant with experience in these matters instructed me. First, stop at a veterinary hospital and pick up some Kitten Milk Replacement formula with a nursing bottle. Next, when I got home, assemble a sturdy carton, a few cloth towels and rags, a supply of paper towels, one or two soft toys, and an electric heating pad (though a hot-water bottle could substitute). Keep the kitten as warm as possible.

A little later the assistant herself arrived at my house and showed, step by step, what to do: Warm the milk formula to room temperature. Set the kitten on his belly and put the nipple tip into his mouth. Then slowly tilt the bottle upward so that he can nurse with his head extended and slightly elevated, to avoid choking. Let him suck gradually; when he spits out the nipple he's full. Place him against your shoulder and pat him gently until he burps. Next, stroke his backside with a damp paper towel (simulating his own mother's tongue) to induce elimination, and wipe him clean. Then, settle him in his towel-lined carton, with the heating pad underneath set at the *lowest* temperature, and a soft toy (simulating a littermate) placed next to him for snuggling. Leave him in a quiet, warm, dark room — until it's time for his *next* feeding three or four hours later.

Overnight, I simply couldn't stick to this timetable. Perhaps if I'd had practice getting up in the wee hours to feed a baby of my own I could have adapted to the punishing schedule. But lacking mothering experience, I gambled that the kitten could survive six hours or so between his last nighttime and first daytime feedings — and he did! Otherwise, I adhered conscientiously to the prescribed routine. I became adept at feeding and toileting. The kitten responded by growing briskly. He purred lustily when I stroked him. We bonded. At four weeks, able to lap up his formula from a dish instead of suckling, he was introduced to puréed baby food, then canned cat food. When his teeth emerged he could chew nuggets of dry kitten food. With my encouragement, he learned to dig and cover up in his own litter pan.

Finally, at eight weeks or so, he'd been sufficiently "raised" and my foster duties were fulfilled. He was ready to be adopted. But I refused to release him! To no one's surprise, I'd become too attached to let him leave. So he joined Tim, Jenny and Toby — who all accepted him easily — to make us a four-cat family. The humane group never bothered to ask for any adoption contract like those I had signed for his three siblings. As matters turned out, he was the last pet I ever obtained from them. (Why? Stay tuned.)

He wasn't, however, the only pet I fostered for them. A couple of times I took in pairs of kittens which could be temporarily housed in my guest room until shelter space or adoptive families became available. But these weren't helpless babies; they were at least six weeks old, able to eat, drink, groom and generally take care of themselves. They stayed only a few weeks before being placed in permanent homes. Harry was the exceptional case.

I don't recall how I decided on his name, but it suited him. His coloring was butterscotch-vanilla, a handsome combination that only one other of all my cats was favored with. His personality was strong: feisty, energetic, fearless. He could be willful and disobedient — and, on one memorable occasion, spiteful. It was a rainy afternoon, I was busy in the kitchen, and a restless Harry was pestering unmercifully to be let outdoors. Instead, I shut him away in one of the bedrooms for an hour so that I could concentrate on my cooking undisturbed. When I went to release him, I found his displeasure expressed with an eloquent deposit on the rug.

He could also express his love. While he got along amiably with his fellow cats, Harry was by nature a loner who bonded closely only with me. (Since I'm rather a loner myself, we were compatible souls.) His single-minded devotion probably stemmed from his crucial early weeks, deprived of his natural mother and littermates, with only one human caregiver to handle and socialize him. His behavior with other humans was odd. He'd sidle up to a visitor invitingly as if eager to be petted — but then recoil and snarl when the person reached out to touch him. But he trusted me unreservedly — this was especially helpful in his last years, when I had to ply him with constant medication — and always knew just where I was and what I was doing in relation to him. He had one unique way of showing affection: when I awoke in the morning he'd sit next to my head and wash my eyebrows with his tongue. Since this was the only "fur" on my face, the grooming may have felt natural from his feline perspective.

It's strange. I always remember Harry as my neediest pet. But in fact his need of me was exceptional *only* at the start and end of our eleven years together. Close to nine of those years were unremarkably easy, serene, trouble-free. From summer 1983 (when he graduated from foster kitten to full-fledged pet) until early 1992 (when his first serious illness was diagnosed) he enjoyed a normally healthy and fully active life.

He *did* have two episodes of cystitis — a common urinary infection, especially in male cats — during the mid-1980's. Both were cleared up quickly with antibiotics. I also seized the occasion to switch, permanently, from supermarket brands of dry cat food to so-called premium products. These costlier formulas, sold mostly in specialty stores, are low in magnesium, a mineral that facilitates formation of urinary stones. The urinary health of *all* my cats benefited! Harry's medical record also shows one occasion when he had a broken tooth extracted and another when he was treated for an abscessed fight wound. (With whom had he been fighting? No idea.) Otherwise, no vet visits beyond routine annual checkups and booster shots until he was almost nine. Then, his troubles started.

As with my other pets' ailments, I don't want to burden you with a blow-by-blow chronology. But I need to share the main lessons of the veterinary course I found myself involuntarily enrolled in throughout Harry's last 28 months.

In essence, he was afflicted with two major diseases simultaneously. One was feline immunodeficiency virus (FIV), an infection of the immune system. It isn't as deadly as the feline leukemia virus (FeLV) in cats or the acquired immune deficiency syndrome in humans (HIV/AIDS). It *is*, however, incurable. The only way to control FIV is to treat the various secondary infections it causes with antibiotic or anti-inflammatory medication. The clinical signs may include inflammation of the gums, mouth, or eye tissues; infections of the skin, urinary bladder, intestinal tract or upper respiratory tract; lack of appetite, progressive weight loss, general unthriftiness. In Harry's case his appetite and, later, his eyes were the most severely affected. He was first tested for FIV in January 1992, with a positive result, after he'd begun losing weight and interest in his food.

There's no way of knowing when and how he picked up this virus. A common notion, erroneous and punitive, is that *any* cat with FIV risks infecting other cats and *must* be kept isolated from them. But according to Cornell University and other expert veterinary sources, the primary mode of FIV transmission is through bite wounds. Casual, nonaggressive contact among cats who don't fight doesn't appear to be an efficient route for spreading this virus. So the chances of an infected cat transmitting FIV to friendly felines sharing the same home are considered unlikely. Harry had always lived in close daily contact with his siblings. If the doctors had convinced me that his condition posed a serious danger to my other pets — which would certainly have been true if he'd been infected instead with the feline *leukemia* virus — I wouldn't have hesitated to have him euthanized.

Harry's other illness was cholangiohepatitis, an inflammation of the liver and biliary system. This was diagnosed after he underwent an ultra-sound and liver biopsy in August 1992. The chief sign is loss of appetite (aggravating his FIV-induced anorexia). Like FIV, it can't be cured. But it *can* be treated with an array of medications — primarily, in Harry's case, with the anti-inflammatory steroid Prednisone.

His ophthalmological ailments, in both eyes, were judged to be herpes viral infections attributable to his weakened immune system. On two occasions he had to be rushed for emergency surgery to reattach an eye that was about to burst loose from its socket. (One crisis, after a corneal ulcer ruptured, arose the very same day that Jenny's euthanasia was scheduled. Both procedures, performed by the cats' respective doctors, went ahead smoothly. Come evening, Harry was convalescing in comfort at the hospital. Jenny had been laid peacefully to rest in our garden. And I, though exhausted, was relieved enough to actually enjoy a bridge game at home with sympathetic friends.)

Harry had two other emergency episodes: a life-threatening urinary blockage that required immediate surgery and an intestinal blockage that was relieved in ten minutes by an injectable enema. But the overriding challenge throughout those last years was just getting him to *eat*. His FIV and his liver disease, combined, nearly wrecked his appetite. I coddled him tirelessly, serving him pretty much anything he found palatable enough to ingest: regular cat food, premium cat food, special-prescription cat food, baby food, people food....One unforgettable November evening, after Harry had refused to swallow a single bite of his dinner, I broiled a pork chop for my own dinner. Slicing off a tiny cube of the cooked chop, I tried offering it to Harry — and *he ate it*. Another little piece ...then another... still another, until lo! my entire main course had been devoured by my cat. I was so happy in my hunger! For dessert, he even consumed a few chunks of cheese.

On my bookshelf Harry has a memorial album all to himself

— most of my other departed pets share one with a companion — because his medical documentation alone almost fills up a notebook. Over three dozen non-routine veterinary bills itemize tests, procedures and charges. Then there are 23 single-spaced pages of my own notes on his condition and copies of correspondence with doctors. A day-to-day log of his food intake and medications, from late March 1992 until mid-April 1994, fills an additional 29 pages.

The array of Harry's prescribed medications was in itself a learning adventure. The anti-inflammatory Prednisone, stimulating his desire to eat, became almost indispensable to his survival. There were also antibiotics (Clavamox, Baytril, Chloramphenicol), appetite boosters (Periactin, Serax), a vitamin to aid blood clotting (Synkavite), plus assorted ointments and drops for his ailing eyes (Vetropolycin, Viroptic, Gentocin, Durafilm).

He had quite an array of doctors, too. His primary veterinarian, a superb diagnostician, performed countless tests and several types of surgery on him. Additionally, he was examined and treated by a gastroenterologist, an ophthalmologist and a specialized diagnostic lab. Their services all entailed many long hours of car travel and much out-of-pocket expense. Probably the least helpful consultation was with a young veterinarian at New York's prestigious Animal Medical Center. After our arduous full-day trip, this "expert" did nothing more for Harry than recommend further tests, all performed elsewhere.

Given his unrelenting, incurable afflictions, I actually didn't expect Harry to live too long. When the end came he hadn't yet reached a terminal stage. But he was so debilitated that I doubt he had much quality time left.

One crisp, brilliant April morning — seven months to the day after Jenny was put to sleep — my doorbell rang. A young woman stood on the stoop holding Harry's blue collar with its tag. Her name was Gretchen and she worked at a local veterinary hospital (one that I didn't then use myself but switched to a few years later). Driving down the street, she had come upon Harry's body in the road, in front of my next-door neighbor's house. She stopped; tried the neighbor; learned the cat belonged to me; was given a carton in which to place him; then came over to impart the sad news to me.

Harry had received a crushing blow to his head and must have died instantly where he fell. (This was *exactly* the same thing that would happen to Toby just four months later.) I thanked Gretchen for her compassion and thoughtfulness; she didn't even want me to look at my dead pet before I buried him. Then, I immediately changed into my work clothes and went out to the garden to prepare a grave for him.

I also thanked the fates, as I dug, for Harry's swift and merciful release. Suddenly his sufferings were over. Despite his infirmities, his life had been blessed with happy and buoyant moments right up to the end. Just a day or so before his death, I recalled, I'd spotted him at the far end of the yard relieving himself in the mulch surrounding some shrubs. After covering up, he sprang gleefully straight up into the air. Then he raced back across the lawn to the house for one more bite of his unfinished breakfast.

Yes, the long ordeal of catering to his frailty had indeed been worthwhile. Though Harry became more of a patient than a pet; though his violent end was as much a release for me as for him; though other sick cats also needed my attention; though I doubt if I'd ever want to go through it again… I still wouldn't have missed our final time together.

A few excerpts from my single farewell letter to him:

"*The shock was horrendous, of course, and I had a good cry before I buried you.… But even that same day (it was a gorgeous spring day), and in the two days since, I took comfort in many consoling thoughts: You didn't suffer! Your end was instant oblivion. I'm the one to suffer, but I can live with it.*

"*You were spared a slow, miserable decline …. The best we could hope for was remissions. Already, these past weeks, your appetite had deteriorated again. No, you were far from terminally ill and needing euthanasia. But if an accident had to put a stop to your potential long-drawn-out physical suffering, I'll accept that it was sooner rather than later without feeling too cheated of your presence.*

"*After all, together we did give you two full years of active, enjoyable life since you first fell ill.….. And let's not forget that you lived 11 full years. Not a 'complete' life span, but well into late middle age. And, my beloved little boy, it was a good life!*"

With Harry, the loner who demanded so much pampering, I felt a rare intimacy and mutual need. Our relationship *was* more special than most others.

· 12 ·

Lucky
Almost to the End

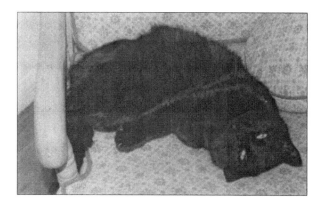

The neighborhood stray who joined my cat family in March 1985 had two unforgettable distinctions. First, he inaugurated a new (if not lasting) way of acquiring my pets. Second — well, I'll save that for later.

Up to then, every one of my cats since Tiger, the laundress' kitten my mother brought home to me as a child, had been actively sought out and selected. Supan, my sealpoint Siamese, was purchased from a private family which had advertised her in the Embassy newsletter. The others were all adopted from shelters I visited to look for a pet. But I never sought to adopt this new cat. He, and my next two, came in — so to speak over the transom.

Lucky's unsolicited arrival put me, for the first time, in the national mainstream. American pet owners acquire *most* of their cats passively. (But they actively seek out more than half of their pet dogs.) A 1998 survey of owners by the American Pet Products Manufacturers' Association revealed that the overwhelming majority of their cats had either been taken in from friends or relatives, or rescued as strays, or born to a cat already living in the home. Only 18 percent had been adopted from shelters and less than 10 percent purchased from breeders or pet stores. I haven't seen an update of that survey, but I'd be surprised if the proportions have changed much.

With me, however, passive acceptance of a pet has been the exception. I cherish my free choice and control too much! (Remember the disastrous episode of the unwanted-kitten birthday gift?) I like to pick my own moment to take on the responsibility of a new cat — then shop around for the particular cat that will best suit. Be reassured, I'm always prepared to rescue an orphan animal in acute need. This *doesn't* mean, however, that I'm prepared to add the animal permanently to my own home!

Nor am I willing to take open-ended care of an open-air "pet" that hangs around outside the house but never comes indoors. Some generous-hearted people I know do. They'll commit to regular outdoor feeding of a seemingly homeless cat — maybe feral, maybe friendly. Is the animal really "wild" or just very fearful? Is it a genuine stray, or just a neighbor's free-roaming, freeloading pet? The dedicated caregiver may never find out, but keeps up the feeding selflessly — indefinitely if need be.

Here's a selfish admission: the few occasions that I *have* taken in strays, or accepted a needy animal from friends, have discouraged me from wanting to repeat the experience. These next chapters will explain why.

Back to early 1985. That was when Tim, my longhair, decided after four years to desert his home and move in with another family. During the winter I'd often glimpsed a solid-black cat hanging around our yard. It gazed wistfully toward the house but wouldn't come near and couldn't be approached. It wore no collar (of course!) and I knew it didn't belong to any of my immediate neighbors. The nights were bitter and the poor creature must have been hungry as well as cold. I took pity on him (or her).

So, one day soon after Tim moved out, I borrowed a trap from my humane group. After dark I baited it with a can of aromatic fish and set it on my screen porch with the outer door propped open. An hour or so later, voilà! The black cat was snugly imprisoned. Before releasing him in my heated basement, I lugged the full trap downstairs and prepared overnight quarters: fresh water, dry cat food, a litter box, some soft bedding near the furnace. Rescue accomplished. What now?

Next morning when I went down I was greeted by a strong odor of cat pee and no sign of the captive cat. Eventually I tracked him to his hiding place, packed him into a proper cat carrier, and drove him off to my vet's to be checked over. Beside the visible evidence of his male gender there were two other clues: the powerful urine smell produced by testosterone, and the fact that more male than female cats have constitutions rugged enough to survive Northeast winters without shelter. The doctor found him to be young, probably from the previous year's kitten crop, apparently healthy and — surprise! — adequately nourished. I left him overnight at the hospital to be neutered and vaccinated.

Now, I apologize for my faulty memory. I can't recall exactly what led up to my finding out the cat's recent history. Here's what likely happened: I brought him back from the animal hospital to stay with me, at least temporarily, until I learned how suitable a pet he might be — whether for me or some other adopter through the humane group. For a while I kept him confined inside the house. Then I let him outdoors, wearing a collar with an ID tag. (An extra tag from some other pet; no matter, so long as it carried my phone number.)

Soon after that I had a phone call from a schoolteacher named Linda who lived not far away. Turns out she had been feeding the black stray regularly, all winter, on her outdoor deck. She couldn't allow him indoors for a good reason; I think her own pet wouldn't tolerate it. She'd missed seeing him for a few weeks and worried that something bad had happened to him. Then he suddenly re-appeared at her house, collared and labeled with my phone number. *What* was going on?

I was happy to reassure Linda. She could stop dishing out food on her deck! I'd taken on full responsibility for the cat: meals, shelter, health care, eventual placement in a permanent home — either with me or another qualified adopter.

Pretty much by default, my own home became his. There seemed no particular reason to send him away. I'd become accustomed to caring for four cats ever since Harry's arrival two years earlier. Now, Tim's defection from the quartet had left a vacancy. The remaining pets — Jenny, Toby and Harry — weren't thrilled to have a stranger move in (what incumbent cat ever is?), but they tolerated his presence without protest.

And the little stray adapted easily to the life of a house cat. He may have been homeless up to then but — thanks to Linda's kind attentions — he was emphatically not "wild." While timid and not too intelligent, he was friendly, undemanding, eager for acceptance and affection. Encouraged by me, he learned to share a twin feeding dish with Harry and to perform neatly in the litter boxes. Without much pondering, I settled on the name "Lucky." This was partly defiance of the folk superstition about black cats, partly recognition of how truly fortunate he'd been to come in from the cold to my baited trap.

My relationship with Lucky was fairly long — longer than with Lucy or Rosalie or Tim. Oddly, though, he left very little impression during the seven and a half years he lived with me. No vivid anecdotes! Here's how I characterized him in a note for cat sitters:

"Little black peasant. The newest, the youngest, the fattest, the dumbest. Low man in the pecking order and knows it. But he's sweet, gentle and *very* vocal. Always notices when you're petting another cat and mews for His Share. *Never* reach out your hand into his face; guaranteed to send him fleeing. *Always* let him approach *you* — unless he's rolling ecstatically on his back asking for a tummy rub. Likes your lap when you watch TV. Loves to have his head rubbed. If for any unfortunate reason you must take him to the vet, put plain newspaper (no towel) in the carrier and try not to feed him before going; he's a bad traveler and almost always defecates or throws up in transit!"

And from my own summing-up of Lucky in his memorial album: "Treated with benign contempt or indifference by the other cats; with patience and moderate affection by me. Pathologically shy and perpetually fearful. Not very bright, but playful, gentle and cuddly....Not a jealous, mean bone in his body. Sweet but hard to handle and do things for because of his uncontrollable flight instinct."

Physically, he was overweight and lazy yet kept healthy. His skin, like Tim's, suffered an allergic sensitivity to flea bites, but a year-round flea collar kept the condition under control. Once every year I drove him the 25-mile round trip to the veterinarian for his routine checkup and revaccinations. And every return drive produced an accident to be cleaned up in his carrier! Fortunately for both of us, he needed few other medical visits.

Lucky, in sum, was a nice but not particularly interesting pet.

My most powerful memory, by far, is the tragic ending to his life. Even today, so many years later, I'm overwhelmed with anguish when I think of how he suffered.

The drama began late on a Saturday afternoon, the first day of August 1992. From my kitchen, I heard the ear-splitting screech of a catfight just outside. I stepped out and clapped my hands to call the troops to order. What on earth were they shrieking about? Then, I spotted a small gray cat — a stray I'd seen lurking around our premises for months — who sprang apart from the melée and sped off into the woods. At the same moment I also glimpsed Lucky, racing headlong away from the house in a different direction. He vanished from sight.

Obviously, with his instinctive fears and flight reflex, he'd been spooked by the noise and nastiness of the fracas. (I never knew which one of the five cats — my own four or the gray intruder — had startled me with that piercing scream.) I expected Lucky to lie low for a while to calm down, then come home when whistled in for dinner. But no. He never came back that night… or the next day…or the day after that.

Gradually it dawned on me that his continued absence was abnormal. Lucky couldn't be "lost" in the conventional sense of wanting to find his way home and not being able to; he knew our neighborhood far too well after all these years. He could have met with some mishap — struck by a car? fallen down a cellar? mauled by an animal? Perhaps he'd succumbed to a stroke or heart attack from his fright? In these cases, why had no one yet found him and called my phone number on his ID tag? Or, could he have been so traumatized by his terror at the catfight that he was *deliberately* keeping away?

After a few days of calling him for every meal, and again late every evening when it was quiet, I set out actively to look for him. I made up a "MISSING CAT" poster and tacked copies to bulletin boards and utility poles throughout the area. I placed an ad in the lost-pets classified section of our local weekly. I systematically rang all my neighbors' doorbells, showing them Lucky's photo (with his conspicuous yellow collar *and* flea collar) and leaving them my phone number. I looked for his body in the brush of nearby woods and hedgerows. I walked slowly through nearby fields, including one 12-acre former potato farm, calling and whistling for Lucky in the stillness of the August afternoons.

To no avail! After he'd been missing a full two weeks, I was half-convinced that the worst had happened. I sat down and wrote him a tentative farewell. It read, in part:

"GOODBYE TO LUCKY (?)

"Are you really gone for good, Lucky Boy? Will I never see you again, alive or dead? Will I ever learn somehow what has happened to you? It's hurtful not to know.

"No one has kidnapped you, of that I'm sure. And after seven years and four months of living with you, I know you well enough to be convinced that you're simply incapable of wandering into a new household to live. You're too timid with people, after all this time.

"As I've said to many friends, I don't really miss your company. But I am distressed by the idea that you may have

suffered, or may still be suffering — if you're trying to live off
the land somewhere. (You were never much of a hunter.) You
were the cat I was least attached to, but I would so welcome
reassurance that you haven't ended in agony. If you did turn up
again, I'd be glad to have you back!

"You had a pretty decent life here, my little black flake, with
your adopted mum and three siblings. Please be at peace now."

Three weeks after this was composed, I had a phone call from
my neighbor Jane across the street. Her husband, Dave, had found
the body of a black cat beside an unpaved road on their property
used for service buildings in the family's business. Was I missing
a pet? Jane knew I kept cats, and this one was wearing a collar.
Dave was willing to bury it if I didn't want to come see it.

Of course I went over to look. Of course it was Lucky. This
was five weeks to the day after he disappeared. He hadn't been
dead more than a day or so; flies were buzzing around his body
but it wasn't yet stiff. He had lost so much weight that one entire
front leg had become jammed through his loosened flea collar.
The collar had gouged a hideous, festering gash in his armpit.
Was it this infected wound that finally killed him? Or was it the
long, slow, self-induced starvation, with no food available beyond
a few field rodents he had little aptitude for hunting?

When I lifted his once-chunky body, he felt so pathetically
light. To think I used to address him fondly as "my tub of lard!"
And to think that all these agonizing weeks — even while I'd
been canvassing and calling for him in the open field right next
to where he was found — he'd been cowering just a stone's throw
away from us, too pathologically afraid to rejoin his home.

In effect, my pet committed suicide.

That evening, after burying him, I wrote him once again:

"YES, A FINAL GOODBYE TO LUCKY

"My poor, pathetic, neurotic little black flake. You did, after all, suffer — for virtually an entire month. The pain is knowing that you were too terrified (WHY?) to come back across…the street to your easily-found home of seven-plus years, and opted instead to live the wild life you'd had next to no experience of. My poor, dear, self-destructive boy. Finally, I wept for you.

"Now you're back — forever — at the home you fled. But you're safe and quiet, nestled under the eastern side of the big black pine, not far from Lucy's grave.…

"Why, why wouldn't you come home during those five long weeks? Did you wrongly think, from that crazy catfight, that one of your own adopted siblings was attacking/rejecting you? Who can read the mind of a fearful, paranoid little creature who never ever felt really secure? Rest, rest my Lucky Boy. Your sufferings are over. And, if it makes any difference, I did love you with compassion.

"P.S. the next day: My poor little lost boy, the more I think about the agony of your last month of life, the more distressed I am. The fact that your fears were irrational — there was NO GOOD REASON FOR YOU TO STAY AWAY makes me even sorrier."

You'll understand, after these outpourings, why my heart still aches to remember Lucky. Self-inflicted, meaningless suffering is no less heartrending than the unavoidable kind. There's just one sliver of a silver lining to comfort me. Of Lucky's full eight years, only his early months and final five weeks were unhappy. By far the greatest part was comfortable, secure, loving and happy. His life, almost to the end, lived up to his name.

· 13 ·

Cindy

The Innocent Misfit

The new adoption procedure introduced by Lucky — passive acquisition of a pet, with no initiative and little enthusiasm on my part — didn't last too long. After his heartrending exit my next two cats, Cindy and Chico, also entered uninvited. But neither stayed more than a few months. A third arrival, Travis, who spent barely a week, was never actually my pet at all. He's been allotted a short chapter only because the experience was so instructive. Following those three over-the-transom additions to the household, I gladly resumed the practice of actively shopping for a new cat when I felt ready to adopt one.

Cindy wasn't technically a stray, as Lucky had been. She, along with several other cats, kittens and a couple of dogs, had a home base of sorts behind a shanty belonging to a family that lived like hillbillies. Their pets were neglected almost to the point of starvation. Two volunteers from our local humane group, Emily and Nancy, had been stopping by regularly for over a year to feed the whole backyard crew. Then one day the dilapidated house caught fire and burned nearly to the ground. The owners decamped and simply abandoned their animals, leaving them without any shelter.

I don't recall how the others were rescued, but Emily trapped one young female cat with her three kittens and brought them to a veterinary hospital. The 12-week-old kittens were weaned and ready for the new homes easily found for them. But their year-old mother, once she'd been spayed and vaccinated, was a poor candidate for adoption. Weighing a mere six pounds, she was too pitifully thin, shy and listless to compete for adopters' attention with all the other cats awaiting homes at the humane group's new "no kill" shelter — *if* she could ever get in. Now, at summer's end, their cat quarters were filled to capacity with a waiting list for admission.

The date the vet cleared her for release, mid-September 1992, was fortuitous: just two weeks after I'd discovered Lucky's dismal fate and buried him. Emily knew of my vacancy and asked if I could fill it, at least temporarily, with the pathetic little momcat she'd rescued. I stopped in at the hospital to look her over. So tiny and timid, sweet, quite pretty (gleaming black splashed with white), responsive to gentle attention — and desperately in need of some home-style TLC.

How could I say no? I paid her veterinary bill and brought her home.

"Cindy," from the Cinderella analogy, seemed an appropriate name. Physically, my new resident thrived. She'd already gained nearly two pounds when the vet gave her follow-up shots a few weeks later. As with all new arrivals, I set up private quarters for her in my guest room — separate food, water, litter box and toys — to acclimatize her gradually before giving her the run of the house to mix freely with the other cats.

As I expected, my three incumbents didn't extend a warm welcome to Cindy. Yet it wasn't long before the two males, Toby and Harry, stopped hissing and began to ignore her. In effect they acknowledged that she was now part of their household. But Jenny, alas, could not.

Throughout her eleven years with me Jenny had already accepted, without protest, the arrival of three new cats. All had been boys. Now, confronted with a new girl, she was bitterly resentful. Was it Cindy's gender alone — a potential rival for alpha female status — that sparked her antagonism? Animal behaviorists suggest that the ability of cats to get along may depend less on which sex they belong to than on whether their other qualities — personality, age, energy level — are a good or bad match. Whatever the reasons for Jenny's hostility, she persisted in harassing and intimidating Cindy at every opportunity. Poor Cindy, in response, spent most of her time hiding behind a sofa or under a bed. She'd emerge for meals and occasionally to keep me company, affectionately, while Jenny was outdoors or asleep in another part of the house. But as soon as her nemesis appeared, she'd cringe and abruptly vanish from view.

To my dismay, Cindy began to defecate — regularly — away from the litter boxes. I'd find her signature deposits in the kitchen sink, the bedroom closet and other choice locations around the house. No amount of cosseting, or consulting experts on feline behavior, seemed to help. To add an extra litter box for Cindy's exclusive use would mean segregating her permanently in her own private quarters; *not* a practical option in our small single-story home. I began to think she might be better off in a different home — one with no unfriendly cats to disrupt her housebreaking and keep her fearful and miserable.

As months went by with no improvement in her sanitary habits or Jenny's tolerance of her, I reluctantly gave up on Cindy. The decision hurt. She was a gentle, playful little creature who had by now become sleek and lovely and quite attached to me. After her dismal start in life she deserved a home where she could feel welcome and serene. I could of course have kept on sheltering her — coping with the fracases, cleaning up the messes, hoping for an eventual thaw in Jenny's cold war against her. But, I asked myself, would that be fair to anyone? Why force two ill-matched pets to endure each other indefinitely? Why not accept that all of us would benefit if Cindy moved elsewhere?

But where? Any shelter other than the public pound, which takes in all animals but keeps space open by euthanizing the un-adopted pets, was out of the question. Our area's private humane societies had waiting lists for admission. Even if one had room to accept Cindy, she was a weak contender for adoption. Attractive, yes — but far too passive and neurotic to appeal to pet seekers in the competitive setting of a shelter with so many friendlier, more easygoing cats to choose from.

So I summoned up my best efforts as a copywriter and created a neat little poster, with an enticing snapshot of Cindy, and a classified ad. The poster was displayed in local veterinary hospitals and pet-supply stores. The ad began running in two local weeklies about three months after Cindy moved in:

"Cindy had an unhappy kittenhood; now needs a quiet, loving home where she's the only cat. She's one year old, healthy, spayed, gently playful, affectionate but shy — and adorable."

The first response came from a college student who lived by herself and, while fond of cats, had no experience taking care of one on her own. Thank you, but no.

The next candidate seemed promising: a single mother of two teenage boys whose previous cat had died. On the phone she sounded warmly caring and responsible. But when I arrived at her home I found danger and disorder. Her sons were running in and out through doors just a few yards away from speeding cars on a heavily traveled main road. The house was stuffed to capacity, with no private, quiet space for a timid animal to feel secure. The woman suggested that I simply release Cindy from her carrier and she'd "make herself at home" in due course. Instead, I picked her up and left — mumbling some excuse about needing to visit other applicants' homes before making my final decision.

At that point, I was soon due to leave on a long-planned overseas trip. I had engaged a reliable live-in sitter for my two-week absence, but realized I couldn't burden her with Cindy's problems. So, while she moved in to care for my three other cats, I took Cindy to stay with another experienced pet sitter I knew, named Beth, who had facilities for boarding cats in her own home. Cindy got along fine there: comfortably settled in a spacious safari cage with supervised evening outings, eating well, maintaining good toilet habits, enjoying frequent attention and play with her temporary caregiver.

When I came to collect Cindy after my trip, Beth gave me a lead to a potential adopter. It looked perfect! This was an older widow who had recently lost a well-loved cat. She lived in a quiet, secluded neighborhood. Her immaculate small house was light and cheerful. She had toys and equipment all ready to welcome Cindy, whom she found adorable and petted gently. With enormous relief, I left them together.

Three days later came an urgent SOS: please come fetch Cindy as soon as possible! Apparently the pathetic little creature had spent all her days in hiding and her nights up in the ceiling rafters, crying incessantly. The poor woman was frantic from lack of sleep. Despite her best intentions, she could cope no longer. I could hardly blame her.

Now that the door had slammed on what seemed an ideal home for Cindy's special needs — perhaps the *only* other home available to her — I felt we'd reached the end of the line. I could think of nowhere to take her now except animal control. And given her incurable hangups, the public shelter could mean a death sentence for want of adoption.

Before taking this irrevocable step, I confided my distress to a friend named Louise. Her sound instincts about cats (and dogs too) were the most reliable of any animal person I knew, professional or nonprofessional. Louise suggested that I talk to a particular veterinarian (not my own) whom she knew well and whose judgment she respected. Coincidentally, he was the same vet who had spayed and immunized Cindy after her original rescue.

I brought the doctor's former patient in to see him, explaining the whole unhappy situation. He clearly disapproved of my firm decision to give Cindy up and was categorically opposed to letting any healthy young animal be destroyed. Humble, I asked if he could suggest a solution. He finally offered to take Cindy in as a temporary boarder — with two weeks fully paid in advance — and display her for adoption in his waiting room during clinic hours. Of course I accepted gratefully.

Five days later Cindy went out to a home. Her new family, clients well known to the hospital, already owned a dog and one other cat. In the doctor's words, when I subsequently spoke to him by phone, they were "*real* animal lovers" (meaning unlike me, obviously!) who accepted that Cindy was "difficult" and were patiently "working with her." He gave no further details. But six months later she was still with them — apparently to stay.

Once Cindy had moved away for good, Jenny was glad to find herself the unchallenged queen once again. And I was especially glad for her, as events turned out. While I was away on my trip she'd begun to show the first symptoms of her stomach cancer. In the six months of life now remaining to Jenny, her comfort and tranquillity took priority. She deserved to be spared the stress of a detested rival presence in the home where she'd been a cherished family member for nearly a dozen years. I too was glad to emerge from what had been an emotionally wearing episode.

The ultimate wisdom of separating incompatible pets is one of the two important lessons I learned from Cindy's five months with me. If the animals lack what the vet called "the right mix" of temperaments, we may be able to live with their hostile relationship but can never really hope to improve it. All our patience, sensitivity, previous experience, consultation with professional behaviorists can't be expected to resolve – or even clarify the reasons for — a visceral mismatch between two pets sharing a home. At times we should just recognize the situation as hopeless and give one of them up.

My other major lesson: seeking a suitable home for a hard-to-place pet, one that few shelters would classify as "adoptable," is a frustrating and exhausting ordeal. Failure is likely, leaving euthanasia as the only merciful solution, and happy endings are rare. (Whether Cindy was capable of being happy is moot. I took solace from knowing that at least she landed securely in a safe, comfortable haven.) Avoiding the need for such a formidable chore is, I learned, a powerful argument *against* unplanned adoption and *for* careful selection of a wanted pet at the outset.

Every now and then, however, a veterinary hospital can be of unique help in placing a hardship case. Here's where I was truly lucky with Cindy — thanks to Louise's invaluable tip. If the hospital has enough space and personnel, the pet can be housed there and introduced to potential adopters. If boarding isn't available, the hospital staff can still promote the animal with a notice on their bulletin board and by word of mouth. Clients already known to the doctors are responsible caregivers. A family may be recently bereaved of a pet and receptive to filling the void at home with an animal in acute need. All trust the hospital to guarantee the new pet's health and, if the arrangement doesn't work out, to take it back and try again. Indeed, the last best hope for re-homing a tough case like Cindy may be one of the community's private-practice veterinarians.

I felt more relief than remorse at letting my little misfit go. As I wrote to Emily, Cindy's original rescuer: "I simultaneously feel guilty, sorry for Cindy, protective toward her — and furious that she has caused me all this worry and trouble (and no small expense) over five long months. It's been quite a learning experience too. I'll think twice and thrice before plunging in to play Good Samaritan again."

That last sentence, I'm afraid, belongs in the annals of Famous Last Words. My very next cat acquisition — less than a year after Cindy left — turned out to be an uninvited rescue.

Chico a.k.a. Spike

The Freeloader

When February 1993 came to an end, with Cindy's departure, so did my eight-year experience of keeping four pets at a time. I had no inclination to fill this vacancy.

A quartet of cats had, indeed, been an accident from the start. My sudden charitable impulse toward Lucky had transformed a neighborhood stray into my house pet with unnerving speed — and no genuine desire on my part. Years later, after he'd been gone barely a few weeks, I succumbed to a second fit of softheartedness by accepting Cindy. *Another* pet who needed a home far more than I needed another pet!

Of course I had enough space and facilities for the proper care of four cats. But after my nerve-racking months with Cindy, following the years of lukewarm relations with Lucky, you'll understand why I felt no urge to square the triangle again.

Most important, my core family deserved undivided attention. Jenny, Toby and Harry — my Second Generation — had been a close-knit trio for over a decade. All three were now in late middle age and required continuing medical care of one sort or another. (At the end of 1993 I tallied up that year's *non-routine* veterinary costs. They included, among other treatments, Toby's fractured leg and thyroid disease; Harry's ailing liver and surgeries for a ruptured cornea and a urinary blockage; Jenny's cancer therapy and kidney failure. Their bills totaled just under $5,000 — a small fortune in a community whose private-practice veterinarians aren't known to be greedy.) So from the day Cindy moved out — when Jenny's chronic vomiting already signaled a gastric malignancy — I was preoccupied with giving every one of the three as much time and TLC as I could.

Jenny, as related earlier, survived only six more months. Her death in mid-September left her brothers by themselves. After this loss I couldn't envisage introducing a strange new animal to our bereaved household for quite a while. My two survivors would benefit from maximum stability and minimum stress by having just each other, plus me, for company. If one of *them* eventually succumbed, leaving Toby or Harry all alone — well, then we'd see.

So our abbreviated family continued unchanged from summer through the fall, into winter and the new year. By late January 1994, Jenny had been gone over four months. At last I began to think about a possible new third cat: perhaps a dainty young sister (*no* physical resemblance to Jenny, of course!) who could add some spice and novelty to the lives of my two aging little guys. I perused the notices posted on my veterinarian's bulletin board describing cats in need of homes. I contemplated an exploratory visit to the public animal shelter ("town pound") to look over all their orphaned cats that risked being euthanized if not adopted.

Then, late in the icy afternoon of February 4 — already dark — there was a sudden commotion on my back stoop. Through the glass panel I confronted a large black-and-white cat. It pawed insistently at the sliding door. It peered beseechingly into the warm lighted kitchen, all the while crying loudly and plaintively.

What to do? Inevitably, the memory of my impulse rescue of Lucky nine winters earlier, and his subsequent absorption into the household, sprang to mind. Oh no, not again! But this shivering, piteous creature — lost pet? homeless stray? — urgently needed help right now. Could I refuse?

I *did* refuse him admission to the house. At the very least, that could expose my pets to any diseases or parasites he carried. Instead, I set up overnight quarters for him — dry food, water, litter box, soft towels — in my heated basement. Then I went outside, collected him from the back stoop and carried him downstairs. He was very approachable. A hefty male, sexually intact, appearing well nourished, with a nasty infection or injury in his right eye. I left him undisturbed in the warm cellar till next morning. Then I made an appointment at a nearby animal hospital — not the one I was then using for my own pets.

Here, an explanatory sidebar is called for. When I first settled year-round in the country, the local veterinary practice consisted of two elderly doctors. One was a borderline alcoholic and the other, while well respected, was bordering on retirement. (In fact, he moved to Florida soon afterwards.) Pet-owning friends strongly urged me to avoid them and, instead, take my cats to a "wonderful" vet named Charlie. Indeed, Charlie and his associates were first-rate. His hospital, however, was in a village a half-hour's drive away. So for the next 20 years I was accustomed to making a 25-mile round trip every time one of my pets had to see a doctor. Eventually Charlie himself decided to retire. By then, a highly praised younger veterinarian had opened a practice just five minutes from my house. So I felt free to quit the lengthy commute and switch to this new, accessible hospital for my cats' medical needs.

Meanwhile, over the intervening years, whenever I sought medical attention for an animal that was *not* my own pet — a rescue or a stray — I simply took it to any convenient veterinary facility. (Today there are three of these within a short distance; the local demand for pet health care has boomed.) This was what I did with the black-and-white tomcat.

When I admitted him to a nearby hospital, the vet on duty judged him to be no more than a couple of years old. I asked that he first be tested for feline leukemia (FeLV). If this was positive he'd have very poor prospects and should probably be euthanized. Fortunately, the leukemia test was negative. I then ordered a complete vetting. He *did* test positive for feline immunodeficiency virus (FIV), the same condition Harry had been living with for years. He also had an infected eye, roundworms and several fight wounds.

I asked them to treat what they could, neuter him, then vaccinate him against distemper, leukemia and rabies. While I kept him boarded at the hospital I'd try to find out whose pet he was. Because — whether lost, runaway or deliberately abandoned — he clearly *had* been a family pet. Hospital staff reported him to be friendly with people and at ease with other cats, though frightened of dogs. They called him a "sweetie" and a "love."

I listed his "Found Cat" description in a newspaper ad and with the lost-and-found services for pets. I asked my immediate neighbors if they knew anything about him; two had seen him hanging around their premises the previous week. One tentatively volunteered to keep him as an outdoor cat, but then changed her mind.

The days rolled by. No reponse to my found-cat advertising. No offers to adopt him from visitors or staff at the animal hospital. I myself certainly didn't want to keep him! He wasn't at all what I had in mind as a desirable successor to Jenny. His black-on-white markings, even with his burly build and rough demeanor, were an uncomfortably vivid reminder of my lost love, Lucy. Moreover, being neutered late as a fully grown adult meant that his still-macho temperament could make him a stressful challenger to Toby and Harry.

But I couldn't go on paying hospital board indefinitely. So after ten days I went to pick him up and settle his bill. (One grace note: their office forgot to list the charge for castration — but the senior doctor decided to throw the surgery in free because, he said, I'd "been so good about all this.") The cat needed a return visit in a couple of weeks for booster shots and re-worming; otherwise he now had a pretty clean bill of health.

And *I* now seemed to be responsible for him. Because nobody else would take him I faced a stark choice: keep him as my house pet, or turn him loose outdoors. The latter might be workable *if* he had been a feral cat, or even semi-feral — say, a former pet accustomed to living on his own for a long time. But this cat was so obviously used to living near and being looked after by people that dumping him out in the winter landscape to survive alone was, I felt, out of the question. So *faute de mieux,* he moved in with us.

What to call him? He had the prominent cheeks common in unaltered male cats as well as a rather Latino look. So I settled on Chico. When I took him to my own vet to have his eye rechecked, Charlie guessed that Chico was maybe three or four years old and had probably been living as a "stray tomcat" — sort of a neighborhood panhandler. He was tame because people had regularly been feeding him outdoors. (As my former neighbor Linda had been feeding the stray tom who became Lucky.)

Well, we all guessed wrong. Chico, it turned out, had been neither a stray nor a house pet. He fit into another, quite distinct category.

I learned the truth by accident about six weeks after he joined us. I'd been asking around for the owner of yet *another* male cat — young, friendly, unneutered, unidentified — who had wandered up to my door acting pitifully homeless and hungry. (You'll find *his* story in the next chapter.) A possible source was a poultry farm a half-mile away, across a 25-acre potato field from my house. I was a regular customer there and often saw cats and kittens hanging around the premises. One day when I came in to shop I asked the farm owners if they were missing a tan-and-white cat like the one I'd just taken in. No, they said — but for a couple of months now they'd been missing a *black*-and-white cat!

Could it be my Chico? By then I had a snapshot of him to show. Sure enough! This was their "Spike!" He hadn't actually been born there. One of their customers had brought him in as a rescued kitten a few years earlier and he'd been part of their farm-cat crew ever since. While the crew did mouse work in the poultry sheds, they were fed proper cat food and given a sheltered place to sleep. None were altered or given much medical attention, but all of them were tame and well nourished — as I'd found Chico/Spike to be.

Why had Spike run off? The owners recalled a nasty turf war that winter between him and one of the farm's other toms. A catfight erupted, wounds were inflicted, and Spike fled into the frigid night. He must have made his way all across the potato field, then a paved road, to reach the area where my neighbors first noticed him.

Why hadn't I asked the poultry farmers about him right at the outset, while I was still boarding him at the vet and searching high and low for his owners? For some reason, the idea just never occurred to me. In the weeks following his flight Spike's owners wondered what happened to him. But they weren't actively looking for him — he wasn't, after all, a house pet — so they never advertised or paid attention to "Found Cat" notices. Now, of course, they were relieved to learn he was alive and well cared for.

But what next? Should he live with them or with me? We agreed that the decision was really up to Chico/Spike. He was perfectly free to go back to the farm any time he pleased. But for me to *throw* him out and force him to resume his old life, after giving him a welcoming home for two months, just wouldn't be fair.

Fair or not — that's frankly what I would have preferred.

Chico, I concluded, wasn't really suited to life as a house pet with my other cats. There was nothing objectionable about him. He was sweet-natured, appreciative of attention, adaptable to household routines like using a litter box and staying indoors overnight. Call it a matter of class. He remained a rough-and-ready peasant, genial but short on manners and education, now expected to adopt the genteel lifestyle of the feline *bourgeoisie*. Yet he couldn't help being coarse and clumsy; he just didn't fit in.

Moreover, my beloved Toby wasn't happy to have him there. Once — I have a snapshot to prove it! — Chico actually mounted Toby (after late castration the male hormone, testosterone, needs time to subside). His deviant overture met instant, noisy rejection. Another time Toby assaulted Chico, suddenly, with no provocation. His attack was totally out of character. Was Toby unsettled by his ailments and advancing age, perhaps resentful of this "replacement" for his vanished sister Jenny? Whatever caused it, the fight was so fierce that I had to pry them apart to avert serious injury.

But since Chico seemed content with his new home — at least enough *not* to avail himself of the option, every day he was let outdoors, of going back to live on the chicken farm — I seemed to be stuck with him. As the weeks went by I also found myself stuck with quite a few medical bills for him (on top of my ongoing expenses for the other cats).

Chico's ailing right eye, my vet discovered, was due to entropion, an inward fold of the lower eyelid which causes excessive tearing and irritation. This was corrected by surgery — a minor procedure but still under anesthesia. Next came stiffness and sensitivity in his leg and back. A blood test indicated Lyme disease, requiring three weeks of antibiotics.. A recurring black stain on his cheek suggested folliculitis, a mild infection caused by facial hair; this had to be treated with twice-daily cleansing and liquid medication. Meanwhile, he was re-tested for FIV, once again positive, confirming his weak immune system.

My new pet's medical chart was filling up fast. And I was learning first-hand about some afflictions I'd never heard of. But the major medical development came in May, after Chico had been with me three months.

He'd been eating copiously but also defecating copiously; food seemed to go through him like a sieve. A test called Fecal Digestion Profile, repeated several times, confirmed that he suffered from a pancreatic deficiency. His system didn't produce enough enzymes to absorb all the nutrients he consumed. Though the condition wasn't life-threatening it *was* lifelong and incurable. It could only be alleviated, by adding a pancreatic enzyme supplement to his regular diet. The daily medication would bring his digestion rate closer to normal. Chico hated the taste of the most effective product. So the vet prescribed another, weaker enzyme powder which he found less unpalatable . Both were expensive. And I'd have to administer the treatment *ad infinitum*. As I grumbled in a note on one of Chico's hospital bills: "What a BORE!"

That's how matters stood in July, as I prepared to leave on a two-week trip. When I got home in early August I found just two pets instead of three. Chico was no longer in residence! A *deus ex machina* had miraculously solved our situation.

While I was away, happily exploring the gardens of Scotland with members of my local horticultural group, my friend Sue moved in to house- and cat-sit. Three days after I left Chico disappeared. Sue called out for him, looked around for him, worried about him. Then, remembering what I'd told her about his background, she went to the chicken farm to ask if they'd seen him. And lo! there he was! Once again he'd become Spike, comfortably settled back in his old rustic digs. Entirely of his own free will, he'd chosen to resume his old identity and life as a farm cat.

But why did he wait so long? He could have gone back any time. Instead, for five and a half months, he'd been shamelessly freeloading on my hospitality and veterinary account. When I left on my holiday, the sole change in our home was the person dishing out his food. Had he been too rigidly set in his ways to adjust to even that small difference in his domestic surroundings? Had he secretly formed such an attachment to me — if so, *who knew?* — that my sudden, incomprehensible absence was rejection enough to drive him away? Whatever his motives, Chico/Spike was clearly satisfied with his choice. He never again strayed from the farm. He spent many more contented years there until finally done in by a speeding car, by which time he was quite elderly. I'd given the farm family a recap of his medical record, including dates he was due for booster vaccinations, but I doubt that they followed up on it much. They *did* tell me they found him much more relaxed and amiable company since he'd been neutered. Occasionally when I stopped in to buy chicken or eggs I'd see him, lounging lazily near the farm's retail shop. He must have remembered me — but neither approached nor avoided me. For my part, I made no overtures to him beyond a casual wave of greeting. After all, the ingrate never once saw fit to wend his way back across the potato field to visit with me even briefly for old times' sake!

My reactions to our six-month association were mixed. I was embarrassed by the whole "rescue" scenario, which cast me in the role of kidnapper of an animal belonging to neighbors I liked and respected. Yet I was also a bit annoyed that the neighbors, aware that their animal was missing, had failed to learn of my efforts to locate his owners. I was heartily annoyed at having been exploited so long by a panhandling "orphan" who already had a perfectly decent home. But I'd also developed a sneaking fondness for him — greeting *"Chico bonito! mi gran gatito"* with a welcome hug when he came in for dinner — and was glad to see him safely back where he truly belonged.

Above all, I felt immense relief at my luck. I'd been spared a choice between two distasteful alternatives: either keep an unwanted pet myself, indefinitely, or recommence the Cindy ordeal of seeking another place for him. I was liberated! So was dear, aging Toby. He had only a few weeks left now, and they were blissfully free of stress.

By some miracle, my departure for Scotland triggered the perfect quick fix. What if I hadn't gone away then? How long would it have taken — if ever — for Chico to revert to Spike again?

· 15 ·

Travis
Just in Transit

My bookshelf holds a group of looseleaf notebooks devoted to the cats who have lived with me since 1975, starting with Lucy and Rosalie. All but two of the books are labeled "In Memory" of pets now deceased. These contain the cats' photo albums, adoption papers, short bios, noteworthy events, medical records, photocopies of grave markers, condolence letters to me, my own farewell messages to the departed, other memorabilia.

A separate album displays pictures worth keeping of my "Current Cats." And one more book, "Temporary Cats," holds photos and notes on the pets that stayed with me for a limited time before moving on — alive and well — to other homes. Tim, Cindy and Chico, whom you've met, fill the bulk of this album. One additional page, headed "Guests," shows cats who briefly lodged with me but were never considered as my own pets. Pictured here are some foster kittens I housed until the local humane group found adoptive homes for them, plus three snapshots of an engaging young fellow named Travis.

The short story of this tan-and-white teenager — his color and markings almost identical to Harry's — featured a pretty long cast of characters. In addition to myself there was another Susan, her housesitter Imana, her friend Martha and Martha's children, our mutual neighbor Chuck and *his* wife and children, plus Laura the veterinarian. The whole episode lasted less than two weeks. But it provided a perfect textbook lesson on the value of pet ID.

I'll admit to being a tireless crusader (and something of a long-winded bore) on this subject. Bear with me, please, while I run through the basics here. Proper identification — easily visible, clearly legible — of every dog and cat is such a *simple* ounce of prevention. Yet it can avoid such devastating losses and achieve so many happy reunions between missing pets and their owners.

It's so absurdly easy to equip any dog with some type of ID. A collar or harness is needed for its leash, after all. *And* the law in every state requires that it be issued a license — which comes with a numbered tag. OK; let's concede that too many dog owners ignore the law and never bother to apply for a license. But they surely have occasion, at least once in their pet's lifetime, to visit a veterinarian. The doctor will unfailingly urge them to have the dog vaccinated against rabies — certified, again, by a numbered tag. With one or the other label attached to its collar, the dog's home can now be located, if necessary, through animal control or veterinary hospital records. Nevertheless, the fastest and easiest aid is always a *personalized* tag engraved with the owner's phone number(s). This can be purchased at minimal cost through any hardware or pet-supply store or veterinarian's office.

Why, then, isn't every owned dog in the country wearing identification at all times? We hear excuses, excuses. The collar and tag may have been "temporarily" replaced with a Christmas ribbon or some other decorative neckwear. A joke among humane workers in my area is that the reason we see so many dogs running naked is because they're so immaculately clean. They've all "just" been bathed, according to their owners, and will be dressed in their collars again when dry.

Cat collars are a different story. More nonsense is heard on this subject than one would expect from some professionals who seem to subscribe to it. It's said that cats "don't like" wearing collars. (Who does?) It's said that they "can't keep them on." (Nobody can, if they're fastened too loosely or insecurely.) It's said that collars "get snagged" on protruding branches or even the cat's lower jaw, resulting in entrapment or strangulation. (Again, this can only happen when a collar is too loose.) So, contend innumerable owners, there's no point even attempting to collar their cats. Indeed, among cat owners responding to one survey by the American Pet Products Manufacturers' Association, only 28 percent had purchased a "decorative" (non-flea and tick) collar for their pets. How many of these, if any, were used to display ID wasn't mentioned.

The medicated flea and tick collar is, in any case, unsuitable for tag-bearing because it *must* be worn loosely enough to keep the insecticide from irritating the animal's skin. Moreover, less toxic and more effective anti-parasite products than these collars are now widely available. (My own choice for some years has been Frontline.) A popular alternative is the elasticized or "breakaway" cat collar. Though these quick-release models now predominate in the stores, they don't seem to me to be the best solution. After all, if a collar is expressly designed so that the animal can easily pull free of it, doesn't that nullify its main purpose as a reliable ID carrier?

What I've found works better, instead, is a sturdy leather or nylon collar with a prong and holes, fastened *snugly* enough that just two fingers can be inserted between it and the cat's neck. Or alternatively, a *slightly* elasticized safety collar with adjustable length and a two-part clasp that snaps firmly shut. These collars won't choke and won't get caught on anything. In my experience over the years, only rarely has a pet managed to divest itself of its collar — and I blame myself for thoughtlessly leaving it too loose-fitting. Now, as insurance against future oversight, I order a duplicate of every ID tag.

What kind of tag should a cat wear? The choices are more limited than for a dog. Any cat that goes outdoors should of course be vaccinated against rabies. But a rabies tag suited for dogs is too hefty for most cats to tote around on their necks, and a tag sized for cats is too tiny to be conveniently read. As for license tags, very few jurisdictions presently issue them for cats. But simply to help an owner recover a missing pet, any legible ID will do. For cats, just as for dogs, the simplest and most time-saving label is still the *personalized* tag engraved on stainless steel or heavy-duty plastic. This can be ordered by mail through stores and animal hospitals, or bought from vending machines in some major retail chains. What to engrave? For all pets, the priority item is the owner's *phone number(s)*. That means home, cell, workplace, weekend getaway — anywhere a family member can be reached any time — with answering machines to record emergency messages. All other information on the tag is optional. Pet's name, family's name, city and state can usually fit on one side of the small tags for cats.

All my cats have always worn ID, indoors and out. The single brief exception was while one pet was healing from an allergic reaction to a collar that had chafed the skin of his neck. So far, the only times the tags actually served to reunite me with cats found away from home were both tragic: when Harry, then Toby, were killed by cars and discovered in the road by strangers. (I shudder to think if they had *not* been labeled as pets with an owner to contact! Their bodies would probably have been carted off anonymously to the landfill in a town sanitation truck. And I would never, *ever* have known what happened to them when they failed to come home!) Short of disaster, I can imagine a pet wandering astray, injured, or trapped in some confining spot — and take reassurance from knowing that his conspicuous little steel tag can help bring him back to me.

There are times, it's true, when tagged collars can vanish — either accidentally discarded or deliberately removed. What then? For added security, it's prudent to equip a tagged pet with backup ID: *permanent* information that can't slip or be taken off. The two options are tattoos and microchips. Both have advantages and also drawbacks. I won't go into the details here; your veterinarian can explain if you're interested.

The microchip has become quite popular, especially among owners of purebred dogs. But for the typical cat that never wanders far from home, a microchip implant probably has more psychological value for the owner than practical benefit for the pet. The chip's presence (under the skin between the shoulder blades), and its identifying number, can be detected *only* by a special scanner available to animal shelters and veterinary hospitals. So the invisible implant is of no use at all when, for example, your tardy cat turns up to solicit a handout from your neighbor down the street.

Although I myself never bothered to have my cats microchipped, relying instead on their tagged collars, all my recent pets *have* received the implant. That's because the humane society I adopted them from has a firm policy of microchipping *every* pet that leaves the shelter — just as consistently as it sterilizes every dog, cat, puppy and kitten before releasing it to an adoptive home.

Enough preaching! Let's get back to Travis — my latest *un*-identified guest.

He first appeared at the back stoop the last week of March 1994. An intact young male, he seemed healthy, well nourished and friendly. He tried persistently to come into the house. I fetched a cat collar from my collection, attached a small luggage tag with a typewritten note — "Whose pet is this? Phone [my number]" — and fastened them around his neck. Hoping to induce him to go to back to his own home, I refused to feed him, though he drank from my outdoor water dish. After three days when no one called about him, I removed the collar. He stayed nearby and sometimes played with a stray cat which had been hanging around the yard much of the winter.

On April 7 (I wrote down all dates!) the tan-and-white youngster followed me down into my basement as I was putting storm windows away. That did it! I immediately swept him into a cat carrier. Off we went to the nearest animal hospital — again, as with Chico, not my own vet's — where I asked that he be given the same full treatment: first, test to rule out leukemia; then, neuter and vaccinate him. The doctor on duty, Laura, estimated he was less than a year old. He stayed there overnight. After I picked him up and paid his $120 bill (the amount is mentioned to make a point later), I released him into my back yard. But late that evening he turned up imploringly at the door. So I relented, brought him inside, fed him, let him spend the night. Thin edge of the wedge!

He settled in quickly and cozily with my three incumbent boys — Toby, Harry (only days before his fatal accident) and Chico (still freeloading with me). This amiable, self-assured adolescent was so obviously used to being cared for in a home with other pets. But where? And *what* was I to do?

At last, on April 12, mystery solved! My doorbell rang; Chuck, a neighbor three houses away, asked if I'd seen a cat answering this one's description. Bit by bit, I was able to piece together a rather convoluted story:

The cat, named Travis, belonged to a caterer named Susan who lived not far away. In February, Susan had gone off to Florida to ply her trade in the high resort season at Vero Beach. In her home here, with her house sitter Imana, she had left another pet, Travis' mother, then nursing a new kitten. Travis himself was loaned out, while Susan was gone, to live with her good friend Martha. Martha, with two daughters and a cocker spaniel, had recently rented the house next door to Chuck. The plan was for Martha to keep Travis only temporarily until Susan returned in late spring. At that point there'd be an exchange: *he'd* go back home to live with Susan while the new kitten, his sibling, would move in with Martha's family as their own permanent pet.

Meanwhile, after Martha had kept Travis inside her house for a couple of weeks, she let him outdoors and he started to roam. Chuck's own children next door enjoyed playing with him and occasionally fed him. So, after Travis had gone missing for some days and Martha became worried, Chuck volunteered to ask around the neighborhood for him.

Travis' misadventure was pure disorientation. He was barely eight months old, born to Susan's momcat the previous August. He'd been suddenly switched to an unfamiliar new home in a bewildering new neighborhood. After being allowed to run loose he'd simply lost his bearings. Having strayed as far as my premises, he couldn't find his way back to Martha's. In retrospect, he was lucky to have escaped being hit by a car.

Now what should be done with him?

I was determined not to let this scenario play again. The most sensible precaution, I felt, was to keep Travis consistently *indoors* in *one* house — if not Martha's, then I was willing for it to be mine — until he could finally go back to his own home with Susan. I spoke by phone to Martha, then a couple of long-distance talks with Susan in Florida. She decided she definitely wanted Travis to live with Martha until she herself returned in June.

So, on April 17, Martha came over to collect him. I sent him on his way wearing a fresh collar and an ID tag with both Susan's and Martha's phone numbers. Even with this added insurance, I urged Martha to keep him inside. I didn't want to see him come by!

I mailed Susan a copy of the veterinarian's receipted bill for Travis' neutering, tests and vaccinations. Guess what! I never saw a penny's reimbursement of my $120. Travis had been my house guest exactly one week. And no, I never did see him again. This was a relief — though I liked my little transit visitor and wished him a long, safe, happy life with his rightful family. My brief encounter with him didn't teach me much about cats. But it *was* a disenchanting lesson about some of the people who assume responsibility for them.

· 16 ·

Daisy May

The Reigning Beauty

At this point in the narrative, let me clarify the census and chronology.

April 1994 was ending; my cat family was still in transition. Cindy had been evicted over a year ago. Jenny had died seven and a half months earlier. Travis had just zipped in and out of the household. Most upsetting to me now, Harry — a treasure of my Second Generation for more than a decade — had been struck down in mid-April.

This left only my dear, frail senior Toby (resident 12 years) and the roughneck gatecrasher Chico (here less than three months). *Not* a felicitous pair. So, rather than wait a "decent" mourning interval before filling the void Harry left, I decided to look for a new third cat immediately. In effect, I'd restart the search for a gentle little sister that I had been contemplating back in January, just before Chico turned up uninvited.

My search quickly came up with a winner: Daisy. While she turned out to be a gratifying pet in many ways, her truly superlative feature was her face. My biased eyes are accustomed to finding every cat beautiful — but she was unquestionably the fairest of them all.

Daisy's other major distinction: launching my Third Generation of cats. This new trio, well-matched and close-knit, proved the most stable and long-lasting group of pets I've lived with. Daisy was the first to arrive and, after nine and a half happy years, the first to depart. My most enduring recollections of our relationship — those I found especially instructive and worth relating: first, the process of adopting her; then, much later, coping with her two unusual illnesses.

By the time I wanted to find a successor to Harry, I needed a brand-new source of cats.

I'd quite had my fill — after Lucky, Cindy, Chico and Travis — of rescuing strays who just showed up and moved in. No more impulse adoptions! No more passive acquisitions over the transom! From now on, I was going to pick and choose my new cats from a well-organized facility: a place where I could actively shop and compare candidates before selecting the most appealing, suitable companion. That meant a professionally run shelter — or possibly a veterinary hospital that helps place orphaned pets. After all, the animals in *their* care need and deserve good homes just as much as the free-roaming strays do.

But one obvious facility was ruled out. I couldn't return to the local humane society where I had volunteered for many years and adopted Tim, Jenny, Toby and Harry. We had come to a parting of the ways — inimical and irreversible. As you might guess, the rupture had nothing to do with their animals. Unfortunately, personnel disagreements of this kind aren't rare among the community organizations managed by volunteers.

So the first of May, a glorious Sunday, I set out to visit an animal shelter in a different community. Though new to me and nearly an hour's trip away, it was well established and respected in the region. I brought a cat-owning friend along for the ride. I didn't need her assistance to make my choice, but sort of hoped she'd find a second pet there to keep her own single feline company. (She did like one cat she met, but declined to adopt.) We introduced ourselves to the shelter staff and were shown to the cats' quarters.

Candidates were plentiful; the season's new kitten crop had started to come in. But I wasn't interested in a small kitten — or in a much older cat, either, that my Toby might not welcome. Among their adolescents and young adults, one beauty instantly caught my eye. White dappled with grey — and the most enchanting little face. She responded warmly to being held and petted. Irresistible! My choice was made on the spot.

They called her Baby. (Shelters usually assign a name to personalize every pet not previously owned — though nearly every adopter changes it later.) Estimated to have been born the previous June, Baby was now almost a year old. Eleven weeks earlier the woman who'd been caring for her, about to move to Florida, had brought her in to the shelter. So — socialized, spayed and vaccinated — she was all ready to tuck in my carrier and go.

But whoa! *They* weren't yet ready to let her go. *I* had to be cleared first.

After all, they knew nothing about me or how I would treat their animal.

Thorough screening of new adopters is a ritual I already knew well and heartily approved of. I'd done quite a bit of it myself, as a volunteer counselor with my recent humane group. But some 20 years earlier, when I adopted Lucy and Rosalie from their big-city shelter, I hadn't been interviewed much about my qualifications as pet caregiver. Back in those days, humane staff were so eager to move animals out of the crowded shelters that they handed them over with few questions asked — and ended up getting most of them back or finding them abandoned somewhere. Fortunately, the shelter profession has come a long way since then. Nowadays every well-run facility conducts an extensive, detailed scrutiny of prospective owners. Some pet seekers find this excessively strict, even intrusive. But the shelter workers are simply honoring their priority commitment to the best interests and safe landings of their animals. A new adopter who respects that commitment may find the interrogation tedious but can appreciate the need for it.

So, as a first-time visitor, I was prepared to spend a half-hour or so in the shelter office filling out their adoption application. Typical questions: Where are you employed? Do you own or rent your home? If you rent, can you provide your landlord's written permission to keep this pet? How many hours a day, on average, will the animal be left alone? Where will it sleep? What happened to earlier pets no longer living with you? etc.

All went smoothly until I came to the "references" part of the paperwork. I knew my veterinarian's address by heart. But they also wanted three — count 'em, three! — *personal* references from people not related to me or sharing my home. Carelessly, I hadn't thought to bring my address book. I racked my memory for names who could vouch for me as a sterling citizen *and* superb petkeeper — and was able to come up with phone numbers for two fellow volunteers from my past humane work. For my third recommendation, the friend who came with me proposed her husband, a retired banker. Fine! I could fill in the reference section. But, I wondered nervously, could I expect my cheering section to all be sitting helpfully near their telephones on this beautiful Sunday afternoon?

The shelter employee said it would take a while to process my application. So my friend and I went out for a quick lunch at a nearby deli before starting our long drive home. Luckily, by the time we returned 40 minutes later, the staff had managed to contact and check every one of my references. *Now* I could be cleared to take my chosen pet away with me! My reaction to the whole process changed from worry to relief — and admiration of their rigorous standards for releasing animals to persons unknown.

I should add that when I went back to the same humane society a few months later for another pet, the formalities moved much faster. By then I was on their approved list and the paperwork was minimal.

Baby was soon rebaptized. "Daisy," a longtime candidate on my roster of names, fit this little ingénue perfectly. I added "May" to commemorate her arrival on May Day. But as with "Jenny Columba," the second name to mark the anniversary served for official use only, like veterinary records. I always called her just Daisy…or Daisy Doll…or Little Beauty…or some other uninventive endearment.

My beauty queen was at once a cuddlecat and a bit of a nervous Nellie. Here's how I described her in a note to pet sitters *after* she'd been living with me nine years:

"She is by far the most timid and skittish of the three — but less than she used to be. She vanishes whenever a stranger enters the house, and rarely socializes with others beside me. She's the most selfish cat, with Pampered Princess aspirations (for example, a low complaining growl if she's chased off a chair I want to sit on), which I emphatically do *not* pander to. A picky eater but I normally refuse to indulge her likes and dislikes. To compensate, she is (in my opinion!) the prettiest of the cats, the gentlest, and the softest to stroke. She's becoming more outgoing and affectionate in middle age; likes being petted but is too nervous to stay put for long. Best to let her come to you, instead of trying to approach her."

At night she came often to bed and snuggled cozily in my midsection. By day, her favorite hangout was my home office. She convinced me that she must have been an executive secretary in a previous incarnation. (Somewhat like Mehitabel, the alley cat in Don Marquis' classic tale, who tried to convince her friend Archy, the cockroach, that she had been Queen Cleopatra of Egypt in *her* former life.) Daisy spent hours napping on my desk chair or the covered typewriter, planting her furry self on papers I was trying to work with, kibitzing as I wrote on the computer or paid the bills. Outdoors, she murdered a few mice and scampered up a few trees — but wasn't adventurous enough to get into any real trouble. I never saw her near the road with its lethal traffic. She was, however, a magnet for ticks and had to be vigilantly checked for these noxious parasites throughout the season.

Given her Princess Daisy temperament, she might have preferred being sole focus of attention as the single cat in our home. But since this was ruled out, she adapted graciously enough to her feline housemates. When she arrived Toby and Chico were still in residence for a few more months. My very last photo of Toby, the night before he died, shows him and Daisy snoozing companionably on a sofa, about a foot apart. She later formed an enduring bond with her Third Generation siblings, Felicia and Freddy (see the following chapters). Initially, though, it took her a couple of weeks to adjust to the presence of Felicia — another good-looking girl the same age as she.

Overall, Daisy's years with me were pleasantly uneventful. Her two most traumatic experiences were health-related. Both were uncommon and difficult, involving expensive care by specialists a long way from home. The first ailment, while not life-threatening, required highly skilled and protracted treatment. The second, heartbreakingly, couldn't be successfully treated. Each entailed a complex veterinary lesson for me — and a bewildering ordeal for my Daisy.

Her health had always been a bit fragile. As noted, she was a fussy eater. Early on she had several episodes of cystitis, an inflammation of the urinary bladder, which were easily cleared up with antibiotics. Then in spring 1999, after she'd been with me five years, her left eye began leaking fluid almost incessantly. My veterinarian detected a blocked tear duct, possibly caused by a virus, and dispensed anti-viral ophthalmic ointments to apply to the eye. Several weeks later, when these had failed to stop the tearing, he referred us to an ophthalmologist. This doctor practiced in a renowned center for veterinary specialists more than 50 miles away.

It took fully a year and a half to resolve Daisy's eye problem.

The ophthalmologist, after examination and tests and a "naso-lacrimal flush" to clear out the mucus-clogged tear duct, pre-scribed medications to give Daisy at home. They helped. *But every two or three months she'd start leaking tears again, and I'd have to resume treating her with eye drops and antibiotic tablets. This looked to me like a chronic condition that could last her entire life. After more than a year, I asked the ophthalmologist to consider an option he had mentioned during my initial visit: the surgical implant of a tube, called stenting, to mechanically keep the tear-duct passage open.*

Finally, this is what cured her. Daisy was checked into the specialist center, reexamined and retested. Then, under anesthe-sia, she was implanted with a tiny stent. During the surgery, the ophthalmologist told me, he found a great deal of infected matter in her nasolacrimal passage. Possibly, he said, it was caused by an abscess at the root of a broken canine tooth; this tooth needed to be extracted as soon as possible.

Daisy spent two nights in the specialists' hospital. She was sent home fitted with an Elizabethan collar to prevent her from paw-ing at her face. She had to wear this obtrusive contraption for four interminable weeks. During those weeks her meals were pretty messy affairs, as you can imagine; each time I had to gently clean her face after she'd eaten. She was on daily medication too. Not long after her eye surgery our primary veterinarian performed dental surgery to remove the abscessed tooth.

Finally, in mid-December 2000, Daisy was ferried on one last round trip to the ophthalmologist (an hour and a half drive each way). He removed the stent and freed her from the hated Eliza-bethan collar. From then on, her eye was fine.

Two years went by.

One day, Daisy developed a sudden voracious appetite. After

a few insatiable days, her doctor ordered a complete blood chemistry test. The lab found everything normal. Perhaps, suggested the vet, the ravenous surge was due to some temporary disorder in her brain. But then her hunger subsided and she resumed eating normally. So we dismissed the episode as a freak, not worth worrying about.

Six months later, in June 2003, Daisy's appetite declined to poor. And she displayed a strange new symptom: disorientation. Her left front leg wasn't coordinated with the rest of her gait and she seemed unsure of the direction she wanted to go. Back to the doctor; another blood profile. Again, the report found no abnormalities.

But this time we pursued the investigation further. Daisy underwent an ultrasound and guided biopsy, performed under anesthesia at the local hospital by a mobile veterinary internist. *This* procedure revealed that her left kidney was filled with fluid and no longer functioned; her other, working kidney was slightly enlarged. The pathologist's report was encouraging in one respect: no malignancy or active infection had been detected in the abdominal cavity. So for now, at least, no treatment was suggested. But the discouraging part: the findings failed to explain Daisy's disoriented behavior, which seemed wholly unrelated to the degeneration of her kidney tissue.

Ten days after her ultrasound Daisy was given a further, very specific blood test, to detect toxoplasmosis. This parasitic disease is easily acquired outdoors by cats if they ingest prey — such as rodents or birds — infected with the protozoan *Toxoplasma gondii*. Most infected cats, however, show no clinical signs of illness. (They can, however, transmit the disease, primarily through their feces, to unborn human fetuses and to persons with weakened immune systems, such as AIDS patients. This is why pregnant women are strongly advised to have someone else clean their cat's litter box, and take other special hygiene precautions, until the baby's birth. According to Cornell University's Feline Health Center, about one-third to one-half of human infants born to mothers who have been exposed to *Toxoplasma* during pregnancy are congenitally infected.) When a cat *does* exhibit clinical disease, the signs can range widely: lethargy, loss of appetite, fever, pneumonia, inflammation of the liver or pancreas, eye ailments, damage to the central nervous system.

Daisy's latest blood analysis, for toxoplasmosis antibodies, confirmed its presence. At last, her illness was identified! She was immediately started on the antibiotic Clindamycin. By the end of July, a month later, she was eating better and another blood test showed the infection reduced. Through August and September her appetite continued good and she regained some of the weight she'd lost. Then, early in October, a new bout of illness. More worrisome symptoms, more tests, more medication. I won't dwell on the details.

But the evening of Wednesday, November 19 is forever etched in my mind. It signaled the beginning of the end. I'd been away from home all day and came back to find Daisy staggering, walking endlessly around in circles. She had vomited, lost all bladder and bowel control, refused all food and drink. As I later learned, the circling and loss of coordination meant the toxoplasmosis infection had spread to her brain and nervous system. By that stage, untreatable and incurable.

Next day her doctor made an appointment for us with a veterinary neurologist on the following Monday. Most of the time until then, she boarded at the local clinic. There she could be professionally monitored, medicated and sustained with subcutaneous fluids.

The neurologist's practice was even farther from home than the ophthalmologist's. After our long drive, my last (goodbye!) time with Daisy was the quarter-hour we spent waiting for the specialist in his consulting room. I stroked and murmured to her throughout — but she was unresponsive, oblivious; not even the ghost of a purr.

The neurologist, after his exam, proposed several exploratory tests. Daisy was admitted to his hospital and spent all the next week there. (Irony: it was Thanksgiving week.) They discovered she had a serious heart ailment *in addition* to the toxoplasmosis and her one weak kidney. Essentially, she was maintained on life support throughout the week.

Just before midnight the next Monday I had a last, dramatic phone talk with the neurologist — who was packing his effects to leave the hospital. An Army reserve officer, he had abruptly been called up to report for military duty. (In Iraq? he didn't know.) His parting verdict on Daisy: her severe cardiac disease, along with the toxoplasmosis, made the prognosis "fairly grim. She's just in limbo, so to speak. Being honest, my guess is that the two problems together are going to make it almost impossible for her to recover."

I went to bed in tears, knowing the only merciful option.

Next morning I heard from the replacement doctor who took over Daisy's case. With no hesitation, I requested euthanasia. Did I want to visit her first? No, I said; her zombie-like condition would make a trip pointless. Nor did I want to come collect her body for burial. Instead, I arranged for individual cremation. Her ashes were duly delivered to me not long afterwards.

The following April I buried the ashes in the garden, under the same spreading Eastern red cedar tree as Toby's and Jenny's graves. (Harry, Lucky, Rosalie and Lucy had all been laid to rest under the big Japanese black pine nearby.) Daisy May's gravestone plaque was inscribed to "My Little Beauty." Her burial date was just two weeks short of the tenth anniversary of her adoption. "I could have waited another fortnight for symmetry," I wrote in my farewell note to her that evening, "but May first looks to be crowded, and today was beautiful and peaceful."

For a perennial memorial bouquet, I dug up a large clump of soon-to-bloom daffodils from the adjoining hedgerow. They were transplanted in front of her rosy flagstone, facing southwest to bask in the late spring sun. Like her, they put on a lovely show.

Felicia

Doing Her Own Thing

With Felicia, two of my hard-learned adoption guidelines were disregarded. For good reason!

One sensible rule — never get a new cat in a hurry — had to be broken, I felt, to prevent Daisy from getting used to the pampered life of an Only Pet.

Daisy, you'll recall, arrived the first of May 1994 while both Chico and Toby were still part of the household. Three months later, at the end of July, Chico (a.k.a. Spike) chose repatriation to his old life on the farm. Three weeks after *that*, Toby's nine lives were finally extinguished by a car. Little princess Daisy was now left as sole cat. Given her obvious yearnings to be spoiled rotten, she simply couldn't be allowed to enjoy this exclusive status for long. So, instead of waiting an honorable interval to mourn Toby (which I would much have preferred), I rushed out to look for a new cat just days after he died.

But I encountered a problem. The shelter where I'd adopted Daisy a few months earlier now had a medical emergency: a ringworm epidemic among the cats. Until the infection was wholly eradicated, their veterinarians had quarantined all shelter felines and placed their quarters off limits to prospective adopters like me.

What could I do? Well, they said on the phone, some new cats had become available for adoption *after* the ringworm outbreak was discovered. These later turn-ins were being temporarily housed with one of the shelter's volunteers, a woman who worked primarily with feral cats. I was given directions to her home and told she was caring for "at least 30" felines I could choose from.

On arrival, though, I found that nearly all her foster felines were litters of recently weaned kittens. That age group didn't suit my needs at all. The choice of adolescent and adult cats was next to nil. One couldn't even be released, not yet having received shots and a leukemia test. A pair of older pets just surrendered by their owner seemed sadly depressed after being uprooted from their home. I felt terribly sorry for them, agreed they should stay together, but wasn't quite ready myself then to adopt two more cats.

This left exactly *one* eligible candidate for my consideration. She was a pretty gray tabby with white markings, maybe a year old — two years at most. She'd been found, along with three nursing kittens in a carton, wandering around a busy street intersection near the volunteer's home. The latter was well known as a cat rescuer in the community. So whoever dumped this little family at the roadside must have counted on their soon being picked up and brought to safety — as in fact they were.

Settled in the volunteer's spacious garage, the young tabby mother had continued feeding her litter for a few more weeks. But three days before I arrived she chose to stop nursing the kittens. Now she was in a cage by herself, vetted and ready to go out to a new home. She was relaxed, friendly, at ease with people. Clearly she'd been someone's pet. She hadn't been mistreated. She'd simply been abandoned by her irresponsible owner when her motherhood made her a burden. So I became her next owner. I filled out the adoption paperwork and tucked the young momcat into my carrier. Besides adopting in haste, I'd now broken a second good rule — pick from a *selection* of pets! But this time, my pick of the sole suitable candidate turned out to be felicitous. "Felicia" lived up to the new name she quickly acquired. She became a happy, bright, easy to care for and enjoyable companion. For the next ten years and nine months, she thrived as a pillar of my Third Generation cat family.

Daisy, as expected, welcomed Felicia's arrival with hisses, not kisses. But after a week or so they accepted each other and settled into comfortable sisterhood. For a full year the two girls lived just by themselves, before a little brother expanded their duo to a trio. Both were about the same age, their coloring and markings in perfect visual counterpoint. Daisy's snowy fur, splashed with gray tabby, contrasted handsomely with Felicia's tabby coat and its pure white highlights.

A nice contrast in temperament, too. While Daisy was self-centered, nervous, timid but eager for cuddling, Felicia turned out to be undemanding, easygoing, calmly receptive to affection in her own laid-back style. She had her personal agenda, her preference for doing her own independent thing — yet she was also amiable, smart and resourceful enough to adapt to most of our household routines. *And* she had a sense of fun. On many occasions after she'd been stranded outdoors in a heavy rain and came home soaking wet, she adored a hearty rubdown with her designated "cat towel."

Felicia's lateness coming home — a regrettable trait shared with Toby, her immediate predecessor — was incorrigible. Though it seemed like willful disobedience, it was really just preoccupation with her own program. Sooner or later, as appetite and activities dictated, she'd make her way home. Eventually *she* trained *me* to adjust.

I learned that when she failed to respond to the dinner call she wasn't ignoring my whistle; she was simply out of earshot. I learned that if I stayed out for a late evening without having first secured Felicia indoors, I'd usually spot her waiting in the beam of my headlights when I came home into the driveway. But not always! On warm summer nights she might doze off in some remote hideaway, not to reappear till the next day. Then I'd find her waiting eagerly at the door for the meal she'd skipped.

Ever since the nightmare of Lucy's death, I could never train myself *not* to worry when a cat isn't safely indoors after dark. As the evening wears on, I'm always tense when the little pink noses aren't all present and accounted for — and, by bedtime, a bit of a nervous wreck. If Felicia ambled in at midnight as I returned from a late outing, I was usually so relieved (thrilled!) to have her home that I couldn't refuse her a little late supper.

Two of her absences were strange and scary enough to be unforgettable.

The first happened in September 1999. She'd lived here five

years and, up to then, never once stayed out overnight. One evening she failed to come home at all. No sign of her the next day. Or the next.…. Seriously worried, I embarked on an active search. I made up a "MISSING CAT" flyer and posted it around town. I placed a classified ad in the local weekly. I listed her information with lost-and-found pet services in the community. I went from door to door in the neighborhood, showing everyone Felicia's photo and leaving my phone number. True, she may have resembled a dozen other gray tabby cats with white accents — *but* she was also wearing her distinctive red collar and legible ID tag.

After four days of an all-out effort to find her, I resigned myself with a heavy heart to never seeing her again. She was attached to her home, I knew. So I assumed one of two things had probably happened. Either she'd been hit by a car and crawled away to die hidden in remote brush. Or, she'd become trapped in some enclosure from which she couldn't extricate herself — perhaps a shed, a well, a dumpster, a basement crawl space — to slowly die there of thirst.

But *eight days* after she disappeared, as I was eating dinner that evening, I heard a sudden commotion outside the sliding door. Yanking open the curtains — there was Felicia! I was beside myself with joy. I sank to the floor and ardently embraced her, carefully inspecting for signs of any injury or illness. But she appeared none the worse for wear. Not especially hungry either. A few days later I detected a slight ear inflammation, but the vet assured me this hadn't been caused by any recent accident or mishap.

Her reappearance seemed miraculous. *Where* had she been? *How* had she survived those eight days and nights? It was one of those times when pet owners wish with all our hearts that our animals could only speak: answer our burning questions! tell us their hidden stories! I never did discover a clue to Felicia's mysterious absence that September. But if I *had* solved it, I might not have been too pleased to find out.

Suppose, say, she'd opted for a change of scene — a vacation away from her home. Could she have invited herself to spend a week as the guest of some cat-friendly homeowner in the area? Such a person would have been hospitable enough to feed and accommodate her — but inconsiderate enough *not* to notify the anxious owner whose phone number was clearly visible on the tag at her neck. (Compare, for example, with the thoughtfulness and concern shown to me by Ian and Frank, my former neighbors, when longhaired Tim turned up at their door and wanted to move in with them.)

Or, on the other hand, Felicia may not have moved in with anyone. Perhaps she found adequate meals by raiding dishes of dry food that some kindhearted people leave outside for stray and feral neighborhood cats. (People like my former neighbor Linda, who provided for Lucky while he was homeless.) I can only speculate.

Four years later, a second bizarre episode. In late summer I went off on a two-week rail trip across Canada, leaving my out-of-town friends Ann and Phil in charge of the cats at home. They had come to stay with my pets many times and knew the routine well. We had no need to speak by phone while I was traveling; I trusted them completely to handle any problems that might arise. The evening I returned home the cats were all there to greet me. But Ann and Phil had a strange, stunned look — and an eerie tale to tell. Felicia, it seems, had disappeared a couple of days after I left. They had seen neither hide nor hair of her for *twelve* entire days and nights. Then, *exactly one hour before I showed up at the house,* she suddenly reappeared. It was as if she'd consulted her telepathic watch and sensed — wherever she was, whatever she was doing — that it was now time to come back and welcome her Mum home. Uncanny.

As before, her physical condition and demeanor were perfectly normal. But poor Ann and Phil were in shock. They'd been worried sick about what might have happened to my missing pet. How would they break the awful news to me when I got back? All I could do was reassure them that Felicia had already pulled this caper once before, on me alone. So her thoughtless vanishing act had nothing to do with them personally. Who knows? Maybe she'd been seized by a primeval urge to "go walkabout" — like the Australian aborigine who treks through the wilderness to trace the spirits of his tribal ancestors.

Whatever Felicia's impulse, that second baffling absence was her last. She never again stayed away longer than overnight.

Her most damaging caper resulted from her most dangerous habit: crossing the street. I could never dissuade her from traversing the road in front of our house to explore greener pastures and wilder hedgerows on the other side. Too often, working in my garden, I held my breath watching her dodge the hurtling cars as she raced across the street to or from home. Because she was fast and agile she was usually lucky.

Then, late one drizzly May afternoon, a woman phoned with a disturbing report. Driving along the road near my house, she had seen a cat hit by the vehicle in front of hers. The offending truck kept going, while the cat ran away into the brush. She herself slowed down, took note of my name posted at the driveway entrance, then looked me up in the phone book after she got home. Was I the cat's owner? she asked. Was my pet OK? What a considerate person! I thanked her and looked around; Felicia was nowhere to be seen. It was now raining heavily. With my umbrella, I went outside to look and call for her all along the street. No sign or sound!

At ten that night she finally crept home, soaking wet, her jaw battered and bloody. Because she had stopped actively bleeding, I decided not to drive her 30 miles to the nearest all-night emergency clinic. Instead I made her as comfortable as I could and took her to our vet first thing next day. Felicia's damaged jaw took quite a while to heal. Her treatment — antibiotics, stitches, extraction of two broken teeth — cost me a pretty penny. But she recovered nicely without major surgery or lasting scars.

Naturally, I hoped this traumatic episode would have one positive outcome: convince Felicia to stay off the road. Naturally, it was a vain and idle hope. She persisted in crossing the street, nimbly navigating traffic, whenever the mood seized her. Deep down, I expected that I'd eventually lose her — as I'd lost Lucy, Rosalie, Harry and Toby — to collision with a car. But my expectation was wrong.

Throughout nearly all of her life with me, Felicia enjoyed excellent health. Apart from her spay surgery (two weeks after adoption, when her nursing milk had dried up) and the injury from her road accident, she saw the vet for little more than annual checkups and booster vaccinations. A persistent fungal infection in the ears was her only medical problem of more than routine interest.

I first noticed signs of this right after her eight-day excursion in September 1999, when she was about six. She was irritably pawing at her ears and shaking out nasty black gunk. After testing for possible ear mites and other culprits, the doctor diagnosed a condition with the jawbreaking name *malassezia pachydermatis*. It's a yeast infection, he explained, caused by either allergy or excessive alkilinity in the ears (fungi thrive in a high-pH environment). First her ears were gently cleaned with mineral oil; then a liquid medication called Tresaderm was applied regularly for up to two weeks. But this treatment, I found, had to be repeated several times over the next two and a half years. Eventually the doctor suggested *preventive* maintenance, once a week or so, with an acidifying solution called Oticlens. As long as I remembered to use it, it kept the condition pretty well under control.

Not until she was eleven and a half did Felicia contract her only serious illness: diabetes. This common glandular disorder is estimated to affect one in 300 cats; middle-aged and elderly animals are more susceptible. With proper management of the disease, many — perhaps most — feline patients succeed in surviving for years. But Felicia's case, alas, proved fatal. Despite our meticulous, tireless efforts to control her affliction, she succumbed a mere five months after its onset.

Those months were, as you can imagine, an ordeal — but there always seemed to be hope. The first month, after initial blood and urine tests confirmed that she was diabetic, we tried a special diet. No use! Then she was started on injections of insulin (a hormone required for metabolizing carbohydrates). From a small dose once a day, the insulin was progressively increased to larger doses, twice a day. Still there was no appreciable drop in her blood-glucose level. Her appetite and energy varied from day to day.

I did copious Internet research on feline diabetes, compiling a mass of technical data and nutrition advice along with first-hand accounts by owners of diabetic cats. Several reports encouraged me to suggest to the doctor that we switch insulin. Instead of the human-extract type I'd been injecting Felicia with for four months, with no measurable improvement at all, could we instead try the classic animal-based formula? The vet agreed and ordered a supply of the recommended product derived from beef and pork. But just as I started Felicia on this, at the end of May, she went into her final collapse.

It was pitiful to watch. For a couple of days she barely moved, refusing food and drink, repeatedly crying out in pain at night. She must have been suffering acutely; cats rarely vocalize their distress. Too anxious to wait until the Memorial Day holiday weekend was over, I rushed her to the hospital on Saturday. Her regular doctor was off duty. The colleague who examined Felicia immediately suspected a life-threatening condition known as diabetic ketoacidosis. Without urgent and expert treatment, it inevitably leads to death. The attending vet's words: "If she were my own pet, I'd take her right now to the 24-hour emergency clinic." So a referral appointment was made for us at the clinic, nearly an hour's drive away, and Felicia and I took off directly.

The supervising doctor who greeted us there immediately started Felicia on crisis therapy with intravenous fluids and small doses of fast-acting insulin. (Her blood-glucose level had soared "off the charts.") She was admitted as an inpatient and I returned home. Later that night the doctor phoned to report that an ultrasound exam had revealed a cyst on Felicia's pancreas. This might explain why she had failed to respond to insulin medication. The cyst was filled with fluid that needed to be drained surgically — but she was far too weak now to be subjected to surgery. So the prognosis was "very guarded." They would continue trying to bring her blood glucose level down in small increments and restore her blood chemistry through drip hydration.

The next day, Sunday, just before noon, the emergency vet reported "no substantive change." Felicia was still receiving "aggressive insulin therapy" and intravenous liquid nourishment. *If* she could regain enough strength to eat and drink and function as she'd been able to only a few days earlier, *then* maybe she could tolerate a risky operation to drain the pancreatic cyst. Any decision on surgery would be up to me, later on.

But barely an hour after this phone conversation, Felicia quietly died. In the doctor's words, "she made her own decision." Right to the end, she was doing her own thing.

Felicia's five-month ordeal was agonizing for *her* only in its brief terminal stage. Until her last days, she continued to enjoy her normal indoor-outdoor life with me and her cat siblings. Though her appetite and weight fluctuated, she remained active and in good spirits. For me, the worst part of her illness was ignorance of *why* she succumbed — when so many diabetic cats like her, diligently cared for, manage to survive for years.

In addition to all I learned about the disease itself, which could come in handy with another pet some day, I gained one hugely important lesson from Felicia's experience. It taught me to be more aggressive in future about investigating and pursuing medical possibilities. Example: When Felicia failed to respond to her first weeks of insulin treatment, would an exploratory ultrasound have detected her pancreatic cyst at an early *operable* stage — in time to undergo surgery that might have saved her life? Further example: When her blood-glucose levels failed to improve after a trial period of human-extract insulin, would an earlier change to the animal-based formula have given her an appreciably better chance?

Maybe yes; maybe no. But it couldn't have hurt for me to be more impatient with her lack of progress, more insistent on exploring alternatives. Ever since, when a treatment is being tried for a veterinary problem, I find myself less satisfied with a "let's wait and see what happens" attitude. If no genuine improvement occurs reasonably soon, I for one am ready to invest whatever

time, expense and research are needed to try new approaches. I
hope my veterinarian(s) will be ready to cooperate!

My attachment to Felicia Delicia (as I liked to address her) was
never as passionate as my affection for Lucy — or for the pet
you'll meet next, Freddy. But she and I were fond companions for
over a decade. I very much missed her easygoing charm and engaging independence. The day after she died, a beautiful Memorial Day holiday, I brought her home from the clinic and buried
her next to sister Daisy, departed a year and a half earlier. A few
weeks later her memorial plaque was affixed to the gravestone.
The tribute reads "Felicia — An endearing free spirit."

· 18 ·

Freddy

Once Again: True Love

Lucy was unique. No pet can ever be that special to me. But of all her successors, Freddy came closest. You might say he was runner-up for Love of My Life.

Why? Can't be explained. One mystifying truth we learn from our relationships, with pets as with people, is there's never a valid *reason* for loving one more than another. A parent may be most deeply attached to a child less endearing or able than its siblings. A pet owner may cherish one animal that lacks appealing qualities found in some others.

Not that my Freddy had shortcomings! We admired, adored

and understood each other wholeheartedly. My house-sitting friends Ann and Phil, who spent many happy weeks with him, called him "the perfect cat." I detected only one imperfection: a tendency to pester — when he wanted to go out, or come in, or be fed, or whatever. (Pestering, let's admit, is a pretty common failing in cats and can be exasperating.) But without this single peccadillo, Freddy would have been a paragon beyond belief.

Another mystery: Why don't I have too much to tell you about our life together? He did, after all, spend almost eleven years with me. But from all those years I can recall only a couple of anecdotes colorful enough to dine out on. Thankfully, Freddy suffered *no* deplorable accidents or mishaps and just one out-of-the-ordinary medical episode (instructive but tedious). Moreover, his sudden final collapse — unforeseen and still unexplained — was so mercifully swift that he suffered a lot less than I did from losing him.

For me, the most fascinating part of Freddy's story is how I adopted him.

Back to September 1995. For a full year, ever since Felicia arrived to join Daisy, the two of them had had the house — and my attention — entirely to themselves. No intruding strays. No competitors for territory. No disruptions to our serene home routine. That was just the way I wanted it, after the unsettled 1993-1994 era of illness and death, drama and disappointment, entrances and exits. But now, a peaceful year later, I felt the time had come to add a bit of spice and novelty: a new little brother for my girls!

The hectic summer had cooled down; the long winter loomed. Local shelters were bursting with orphaned cats and kittens. So I planned a mid-September visit to the same humane society where I'd adopted Daisy and Felicia. A few days before my scheduled trip, however, I took Felicia to her vet for an annual checkup and booster shots. While there, I glanced at some notices on the hospital's bulletin board about pets in need of homes. Pat, their office manager, saw me looking at the ads. I was in the market for a third cat, I told her; did she know of any hardship cases for adoption? Her face lit up. Yes! She started telling me about a five-month-old boy they were boarding — just the young age and male sex I was hoping to find — as she escorted me to the kennel area.

Immediately, across the room, I spotted an adorable kitten pouncing gleefully on a toy in his cage. He had the same cheery colors as Harry had: butterscotch splashed over vanilla. Pat opened the cage and I folded him into my arms. His purr was deafening. As Pat put it, "the motor runs all day."

Well, that decided it. Instant, visceral attraction; no need to shop further. But I couldn't take my new kitten home right away. Partly because of the hospital's responsibility to his sponsor, partly because he first needed minor eye surgery, I could "reserve" him now and adopt him in a few more days.

This was the background: Earlier that summer a hungry stray kitten showed up at a local Italian restaurant called Pomodoro. The staff started feeding him, regularly. Also, because the building bordered a highway with dangerous traffic, they let him sleep in their basement at night. At dinner each evening he would circulate among the tables on their outdoor terrace, making friends with the diners. One he especially charmed was a cat lover named Marilyn. She and her husband owned a second home in the village where they spent weekends and vacations. Over that summer they dined at Pomodoro several times.

As Labor Day approached, however, the manager announced that Pomodoro would close after the holiday. Then, Marilyn worried, what would happen to the kitten they'd been taking care of? Alas, none of their employees or customers were able to adopt him. He'd just have to be left on his own in the neighborhood after Pomodoro locked its doors. In that case, asked Marilyn, would they let *her* take him and try to find him a home? Of course, they said.

So Marilyn stopped by during Labor Day weekend to collect the kitten. She had him admitted at the animal hospital she had used in the past (the same one I myself was then using). There, he was to be boarded, vetted and offered for adoption. Marilyn and her husband would be away several weeks on a business trip. Then, when they got back to town, if the kitten hadn't already found a home she'd turn him over to a local humane society. Meanwhile, she'd cover all his veterinary and boarding expenses. But she asked to approve any prospective owner who wanted to adopt him directly from the hospital.

When I met him, on a Friday, he'd been living there about two weeks. (One staff member later told me that she had planned to adopt him herself *if* he hadn't been taken by one of the hospital's clients.) Over the weekend a doctor repaired his "cherry eye" problem. And Pat, the office manager, spoke to Marilyn long-distance to tell her of my interest, give her my phone number, and recommend me as a dependable caregiver whom they'd known for years. So, Monday morning, I was given the green light to come pick him up.

Marilyn phoned me that same evening. It was too early to tell her more than how appealing I found her little rescue — not even time yet to choose a name for him! — and how confident I was that he'd fit beautifully into our family. His two new big sisters had hissed rudely at him on arrival (of course), but I was sure they'd soon adjust and accept him (as they did). Marilyn was delighted to learn that he'd have other cats for company in his home.

I did have one worry, though. Marilyn obviously cared very much for cats. She'd gone to a lot of trouble and expense on behalf of this little stray. So — why hadn't she kept him herself? Perhaps right now she felt she didn't have time to take care of a new pet. But couldn't she change her mind some day, *after* I'd become attached to him, and decide that, after all, she'd like to take him back to live with her? I dreaded committing myself to love an animal I might, at some later date, feel morally obliged to return to his rescuer.

Marilyn reassured me right away. No, she definitely could *not* keep the kitten, now or in future, for an immutable reason: Her husband was allergic to cats. So allergic, indeed, that she'd been compelled to give up her own beloved cat, Tuxedo (black and white, of course). He had gone to live with Marilyn's mother, so at least she could see him occasionally on family visits there. But as long she shared her own home with her husband, no cat could be permitted on their premises.

Allergies! Ugh! I thought back forty years, to poor Stan. He, you'll recall, was my college friend's fiancé who first learned about his own acute sensitivity to cats from my Siamese in Paris. Ever since, Stan can't tolerate even a short stay in a room where a cat has lived without suffering an asthma attack. I thought, too, about another cat-allergic friend named Karen, who is highly gregarious. She became frustrated with having to refuse dinner invitations from the cat owners in her social circle. So she signed up with an allergist for an expensive course of immunization therapy requiring year-round shots. Thus treated, Karen could at least spend a few hours in a home like mine — though in winter, with windows all shut, she'd still begin to sneeze before the evening was over.

But Marilyn's husband, like Stan, never attempted to medicate himself to resist cat dander. I was eager for her to come over and see Freddy contentedly settled in his new home. But their reunion took a while. The next summer, when windows were all opened for maximum ventilation and the cats could be "quarantined" outdoors in the garden at safe breathing distance from Marilyn's husband, we finally fixed a date for their visit. To help celebrate the occasion, I invited other cat-owning friends to join us. Yet Marilyn turned up alone! At the last minute her husband had chickened out, fearing his reaction to the dander of *three* cats. When I invited them a second time, months later, he was brave enough to come with her. I'll confess, though, we were all a bit nervous throughout our lunch.

It meant a great deal to me that Marilyn could greet Freddy in person again on these brief visits. I felt tremendously indebted to her. The coincidental timing — her impulsive rescue of him at the restaurant; my impromptu meeting with him at the hospital — had been so incredibly lucky for all of us. As one inadequate token of my appreciation, I roughly calculated her hospital costs for Freddy, then mailed her a check to reimburse as much of the total bill as I could estimate. (She protested, but accepted.) Every year, with a Christmas card, I sent her an up-to-date snapshot of her Pomodoro kitten as he matured and thrived. My admiration for her selfless gesture, and my gratitude for her gift of a pet who became so precious to me, can't be overstated.

From day one, Freddy proved a winner.

Besides being adorable, he was bright, playful, resourceful, dependable, adventurous, friendly and unselfish with his fellow cats, unfailingly affectionate with me. One of my special quality times with him was in the morning: I'd finish dressing and start to leave the bedroom. Freddy would sit there gazing at me from the bed — until I gazed right back and gave him a hug. The ritual moment brought to my mind a corny song from an old movie ("High Society," I think), in which Bing Crosby gazed at Grace Kelly while he crooned "*I give to you and you give to me. True love. True love.*" I often crooned this myself to Freddy.

With other people, he was somewhat less outgoing than Toby. (*He*, you'll remember, had been my hospitable Little Man of the House who made the rounds to greet guests and jump into every receptive lap.) But as soon as Freddy became accustomed to a new presence and voice in his home, he was fully at ease and amiable with visitors. I have snapshots of him sitting on my sofa next to a guest playing Scrabble. He appears to be intently kibitzing the game on the board — as if he could devise better words with the same letters. My Scrabble friend, incidentally, had always been a bit afraid of cats; she couldn't explain why. But in the course of many weekend visits to me and mine over the years, her nervousness gradually subsided. Freddy was the one she felt most relaxed with — even volunteered to caress. Freddy himself could be so relaxed with attentive strangers that I had to apologize for him at the veterinarian's. He purred so loudly on the examining table that the doctor had trouble listening to his heart with the stethoscope. And there *was* a slight murmur to listen to; more about this later.

His relations with his two cat sisters were comfortably close if not intimate. Here again, Toby had been unique. So far, with my other pets, I've seen nothing approaching Toby's and Jenny's love match — endless cuddling and mutual grooming — preserved in many treasured photos. Freddy, on rare occasions, would wash Daisy's head, usually when they were cozily settled on my blanket for the night. But she'd put up with it for only a minute or so and never reciprocated.

As my bedmates, the three cats deployed as a team: Daisy snuggled against my chest, Felicia alongside my back, Freddy nestled in the crook of my knee. His most playful interaction was with Felicia —*only* at mealtimes. (Go figure!) While waiting for me to get their food ready at the counter, they'd start to pounce, tumble, wrestle and shadow-box — just like two littermate kittens exercising. Their acrobatics were such fun to watch that I often slowed the meal service to prolong the show.

After breakfast, when Freddy, Daisy and Felicia were let outdoors in nice weather, all immediately set out on their separate ways. (A daily demonstration that cats are solitary creatures by nature, not pack animals like dogs!) An eloquent photo taken by Ann and Phil on one of their summer visits was captioned "Starting the Day": My three pets, having just emerged from the house, are all peering alertly into the landscape, eager for the new day's sights and scents and adventures awaiting them.

On warm summer evenings when I had no social plans, the cocktail hour was a favorite time shared with Freddy and his sisters. To relax after the day's work in my office or garden, I'd serve myself a glass of sherry and a dish of munchies. Then I'd sit down on the back stoop to savor them at leisure. The sun would be setting, the breeze would be freshening, the mourning doves would be cooing. And *voilà!* My little carnivores would all suddenly reappear from wherever they'd been spending their own day. They'd evidently consulted their internal watches and realized that dinnertime was imminent. While I sipped and munched and watched delightedly, the three mature felines would then play together on the lawn like frisky kittens — chasing, cavorting, somersaulting, racing each other up and down the big apple tree. At times Freddy would dash up to settle next to me on the stoop, adroitly managing not to upset my drink.

Those moments were golden.

A virtue I particularly appreciated in Freddy was his helpfulness in alerting me to another cat who wanted to come indoors. At first, I misread his whimpering near the sliding door, thinking he was pestering me to let *him* out. But no! Instead, I'd see one of his sisters waiting on the stoop to be let in. The two would then nuzzle noses in greeting — and Freddy would get a warm thank-you hug for notifying me.

Have I explained, by the way, why I insist on *letting* my pets in and out each time? Obviously this is more trouble for me than simply leaving a window ajar or installing a free-access "pet door." But obviously, too, it keeps my skilled little hunters from hauling their unsightly trophies into the house ("something the cat dragged in"). Mainly, though, I value control over the *timing* of their outings as an essential precaution for their own safety.

Freddy, like nearly all my cats, occasionally stayed outdoors late, choosing to ignore the dinner call. But with a single exception, I could always summon him home before my bedtime. I did this with persistent loud whistling and clapping, sometimes a tour by flashlight around the property. Then, one unforgettable night, he never showed up at all.

Worried, I went to bed imagining the worst, yet hoping for reassurance next day. But in the morning *no* Freddy had reappeared to wait at the door. I went outside and began calling him. Suddenly, I heard faint answering cries from the property next door. This was midsummer. The wild hedgerow separating my yard from my neighbors' had grown almost impenetrably full, choked with weeds and vines and tangled brush. I bushwhacked my way across in the direction of the cries. They got louder and more insistent.

Emerging into the neighbors' yard, I faced the small field

where they planted corn each year. And there amid the alien corn was my Freddy, sitting inside a large cage and yelling his lungs out. Next to him stood the lady of the house, a good friend. She apologized for not having been able to unfasten the cage door and free my frantic pet. Her son, she told me, had baited the trap the previous evening and had now gone off to work for the day. It took only a minute for me to undo the latch and release poor Freddy.

My captive cat had spent the night in a humane trap borrowed from one of the local animal shelters or veterinarians. My neighbor hoped to relocate some raccoons which had been raiding his ripening corn, releasing them from the trap in distant woods. I sympathized with their raccoon problem. But I asked them — please! — to check their trap before retiring each night to make sure no free-roaming pets were accidentally incarcerated.

The episode reminded me of an incident a few years earlier with another neighbor, who lived in back of me. One hot summer night I was kept awake well past midnight by a low, persistent noise through my open bedroom windows. It sounded like a man talking softly, nonstop; I couldn't distinguish the words. Were my rear neighbors entertaining so late? I peered out the window. All was dark in their direction but the murmuring went on. To get any sleep, I had only two options — shut my windows and stifle, or fetch some earplugs from my travel toilet case — and chose the latter.

Next day, I phoned the neighbor. Did he know of any guests or intruders in his garden overnight? No! Seems that he, too, was desperate to keep raccoons from eating his corn just as it grew ready to pick. Instead of trapping, he was trying to scare the critters away with noise. He'd left a battery-powered radio tuned to an all-night news station in the field. Please, he begged me, be patient a few more days until his corn could be harvested. Ah, country life.

As best I remember, Freddy's night in the trap was his most unpleasant experience. On the whole he led a charmed life — and pretty healthy too. He'd always had a conspicuous discoloration in one eye. The doctors decided it must be scarring from an early corneal ulcer, before I adopted him, and didn't affect his vision. He did have a slight heart murmur, detected with the stethoscope during yearly checkups. But as long as he presented no symptoms of illness, his vet saw no pressing need to investigate the matter further.

Only two ailments are recorded in my medical file for Freddy. Both were gastrointestinal; both were manifested solely by loss of appetite. The first, at age seven, was minor. Though tests couldn't confirm the cause it was probably a bacterial infection, since the antibiotic Clindamycin cleared it up completely in three weeks.

Freddy's second illness, two years later when he was nine, was more challenging and costly to diagnose and more complicated to treat. It may well have been a form of Inflammatory Bowel Disease, a common cause of digestive problems in middle-aged and older cats — even though Freddy *didn't* display IBD's two most common symptoms, diarrhea and vomiting. In March 2004 he simply went off his food again — but this time antibiotics didn't help. He became thin and listless. He had X-rays, blood tests and an abdominal ultra-sound. Finally, early in June, he underwent an endoscopy: examination inside the intestinal cavity with a surgical instrument, snipping tissue samples for biopsy. The tests revealed *two* concurrent problems: an infection known as helicobacter, along with inflammation of the gastrointestinal mucous lining.

All through that summer and into fall, Freddy was subjected

to a daily barrage of pills. The most effective one was Prednisone, an anti-inflammatory steroid. This medication helped restore his appetite, weight and energy. By late September he was eating normally and seemed his old self again. Even so, the vet kept him on a lower maintenance dose of Prednisone, very gradually phased out over the winter months. His ordeal appeared over. Yet the doctor warned me to stay alert for possible recurrence of IBD, which can be chronic. For the remainder of Freddy's life, however, he stayed healthy.

But to my immeasurable sorrow, his life lasted only a year and a half longer. It ended with devastating suddenness in mid-May 2006.

On a rainy Friday, after consuming a hearty breakfast, Freddy spent the day quietly snoozing indoors. Yet as day turned into evening he appeared more and more ill. He was lethargic, ignored his evening meal, moved with difficulty, occasionally even whimpered in pain. (It's rare for cats to vocalize their physical discomfort.) He joined me in bed that night, as usual, but didn't stay long. Next morning I found him lying in one of the litter boxes, looking confused and miserable.

Immediately I phoned the vet that I was bringing Freddy in as an emergency. When I looked to put him in his carrier, he had crept under my bed to hide and cried in protest as I moved him. On our drive to the hospital he was silent — but, at one point, thrashed violently in the carrier. After I placed his inert body on the examining table, the doctor could find no heartbeat or respiration. He was gone! The thrashing in the car had been his final death convulsion.

Dazed from shock, I had enough presence of mind to request a necropsy. What in the world could have brought on this instant, relentless collapse? Other than a slightly erratic appetite for a few weeks, Freddy had shown no signs of illness. Indeed, he'd appeared his normal, lively, sociable self right up to his last few hours. Perhaps whatever killed him couldn't have been diagnosed and successfully treated in advance. But I had to seek *some* kind of answer to the tragic mystery.

The attending vet performed the necropsy that afternoon. She saw abnormalities in Freddy's chest cavity suggesting a heart or lung ailment, and sent various tissue samples out for laboratory analysis. The only abnormal finding the lab reported was the pulmonary arteries, which were "markedly thickened, with hypertrophy [enlargement] of the smooth muscle." Several pathologists had examined the slides. In the absence of specific evidence, such as heartworm or a clot, they couldn't agree on any clinical reason for his sudden plunge into death.

So the mystery remained unsolved. I grasped at a few straws of consolation: Almost surely, Freddy's fatal condition couldn't have been predicted or detected. (Unless, perhaps, it had something to do with that persistent heart murmur we never bothered to investigate.) His terminal suffering had been mercifully brief — just a few hours, unlike the protracted anguish of my own bereavement. His eleven years of life, though far too few for my liking, had been satisfyingly full and undeniably happy.

I had hoped that Freddy and I could grow old together, that we'd set out to cross the Rainbow Bridge at about the same time. But if that was not to be, at least he was now reunited — somewhere — with Daisy and Felicia.

Their three graves are close neighbors under my big cedar tree. I'll always think of the trio as a cohesive family unit. For most of a decade they shared an easy, confident kinship. It's true that Freddy was two years younger than the girls, that he joined the household a year after they did, that he outlived Felicia by a full year and Daisy by almost two and a half years. Moreover, by the time Freddy himself departed, he'd been living with two *new* adoptive sisters for quite a while.

Even so — the loss of this pet who meant so much to me ended the long run of a very successful show. Freddy's exit brought down the curtain on my Third Generation of cats.

Queen / "Angela" / Queen
Too Vulnerable to Stay

This cat, like Travis, spent only a week with me. So she doesn't really count as one of my pets. But, unlike Travis, she had been voluntarily invited and *intended* as my pet. The reason she couldn't stay was the fault of others — not mine and certainly not hers. Her aborted adoption taught me about an important and sensitive issue. Thus her story, brief as it is, shouldn't be skipped over.

March 2004. Daisy had been deceased about four months. By then I felt that a new companion for Felicia and Freddy would be acceptable. So I returned to the same shelter where I'd adopted Daisy and Felicia a decade earlier.

At that time of year their choice of cats wasn't large, but one plump and pretty female appealed to me. They called her Queen. She was white with black markings, a sweet face, gentle demeanor. She'd been living with them a full year since they found her abandoned at the shelter door; now they estimated her to be four years old. With more compassion than passion — she truly deserved a good home after being dumped and then waiting so long — I filled out the adoption forms and brought Queen home.

"Angela," her new, dainty name that I'd been reserving for a fair lady, was *very* shy. Though I left the door to her separate guest-room quarters slightly ajar, she spent most of her day there out of sight under the beds. Whenever I went in to serve her food, refresh her water or attend to her private litter box, I tried to entice her into a brief play-and-cuddle session with me. Gradually she grew more responsive and purred nicely when petted.

One day, as I held her in my lap, I suddenly became aware that her front paws were suspiciously soft. While I stroked her she was flexing her toes blissfully — but *no claws* could be seen or felt.

I couldn't remember ever having handled a declawed cat. I wasn't even sure this was the correct diagnosis. So I drove "Angela" to my vet for an urgent consult. He quickly confirmed that her claws in *all four feet* had been surgically removed.

The news stunned me. I was shocked, too, that the shelter staff had utterly failed to inform me of Queen's infirmity *before* I adopted her. What were they thinking? And I was disgusted beyond words with her original owners — whoever they may have been. First, they'd paid a substantial sum for their pet's irreversible mutilation. Then, they furtively discarded the poor little cripple to become someone else's responsibility.

Not least, I was sorely disappointed. Could I provide proper care and a good life for this vulnerable creature, hobbled by her handicap, in a home with other, normally functioning pets? I couldn't see how I'd manage. She'd have to go back to the shelter.

I phoned the executive director there. She too was shocked to learn about the declawing; she'd been away the day I'd come there to adopt Queen. How was it possible, I asked, that in the entire year this cat spent with them, *no one* — not a single kennel or veterinary employee — had noted and recorded that her claws were missing?

This shelter wasn't some giant municipal facility which processes thousands of animals each year. It was a small humane society in a small-town community, with annual intake and adoption figures not exceeding a few hundred. The director was a dedicated, conscientious professional for whom I had high regard. Their standards were scrupulous. Their roster of cats and dogs listed any special limitations that potential adopters need to be warned about — such as "prefers a home with *no* dogs/cats/other pets/small children," "special medical needs," "declawed." Why, then, hadn't Queen's disability been registered and brought to my attention?

The director murmured something about a newly hired kennel manager who must have made a record-keeping error at the time Queen was admitted. As for their veterinarians who had examined and vaccinated her, they must have assumed — wrongly! — that the shelter staff was aware of her impairment and would notify any potential adopters.

You'll agree, I hope, that a declawed cat *must* be an indoor-only cat. Outdoors, the animal is wholly defenseless against threats from any creatures it might encounter. (It can't even escape up a tree with ease.) Could I succeed in keeping just *one* pet confined inside at all times, while allowing my other pets to go in and out? No way! Such an arrangement would be a logistical nightmare. And it would be cruelly unfair to the cat who must remain cooped up alone in the house all day, seeing its companions free to enjoy the outdoors.

Yet when Queen went back to the shelter, I thought, she shouldn't have to stay cooped up there much longer. All the staff need do was publicize her as a hardship case deserving a special break. Somewhere the right, loving "forever" home awaited her. Her infirmity could even be promoted as an asset in a fastidious household — with a family glad to accommodate an indoor cat who wouldn't (couldn't!) shred their furniture.

Mind you, I'm as fond as any homeowner of my curtains, rugs and upholstery. Yet I'm not so deeply enamored that I can't bear living with furnishings in less than pristine condition. As a practical matter, we know that *no* pet owner can afford to be a perfectionist about home décor. Virtually every animal sheds hair. Dogs have housebreaking accidents, cats cough up hairballs, both species have stomach upsets that produce messes. As for cats' claws, every sensible owner should be well prepared to *minimize* their damage. Eliminate it completely? That, I'm afraid, can only be guaranteed by surgical amputation — the outrage perpetrated on Queen — or by substituting a stuffed toy for the live animal.

We humans must trim our nails. Cats must remove the outer sheath of their claws so that new growth can emerge. Their scratching is instinctive behavior. The stripping action hones their natural weapons to peak condition. The stretching against a firm upright surface tones their back, leg and shoulder muscles. The whole exercise stimulates their emotional well-being. It's beneficial for them — and need *not* be destructive for us.

Ever since Lucy and Rosalie arrived, I've always provided my cats with scratching posts. The kind I find most worthwhile are tall, sturdy posts on a heavy base, covered with rough sisal fabric, sometimes rubbed with catnip or topped with a catnip toy, strategically placed to be accessible to my pets. By the way, there's an excellent chapter on scratching posts in a book called *Cat Love* by Pam Johnson, a feline behavior consultant, published 1990 by Storey Communications.

All my pets have used their posts faithfully — if not exclu-

sively. I'll admit having had to patch a few tattered spots on upholstery that I was unwise enough to cover with the coarse tweedy
material that cats most love to sink their claws into. And one pet
is infuriatingly fond of digging into my prize hand-hooked wool
rug. (I'm thinking of putting a flat scratching board on the floor
expressly for her use.) But overall, I really can't complain. The
top-quality indoor posts serve well and last for years. And with
my cats' daily access to the outdoors, they obtain most of their
manicures from nature's own, best scratching material: the bark
of upright trees and fallen logs.

Clipping the tips of a cat's claws is another helpful precaution.
I used to do this regularly, back in the days when Lucy and Rosalie and I lived mostly in a city apartment. After we moved full-
time to the country I kept it up only with Lucy. This was because
she had a loving but excruciating habit of kneading my tender
chest as she snuggled under the bedclothes with me at night. Otherwise — remembering the day that Rosalie, with her neatly
trimmed nails, was helpless to grip herself down from a tall tree
— I don't think it's wise for the vital defense weapons of any *indoor-outdoor* cat to be even slightly disarmed.

Luckily, my location and lifestyle permit my own pets to enjoy
the best of both worlds. But I appreciate, of course, that many
— perhaps most? — cat owners today choose to keep their pets
entirely indoors, for many good reasons. For these cats, snipping
the sharp points of their front claws benefits everyone. Veterinarians recommend it as a regular practice and I wholly agree. But
nail trimming should supplement — never substitute for — that
all-important scratching post.

As for completely removing a cat's claws, you already know
my opinion. An abomination!

On philosophical/ethical grounds, we humans simply have no

moral right to mangle living creatures — least of all the companion animals who share our homes — as if they were lifeless articles of decoration. On medical/psychological grounds, we can't possibly judge how deeply a pet's physical and emotional well-being suffer from such permanent disfigurement. Try to imagine having the last joint of every one of your fingers amputated. That's exactly what surgical declawing does to a cat.

I've seen, in the pet-care literature, feeble attempts to excuse the procedure. The apologists downplay the all-too-frequent discomfort, stress and maladjusted behavior that can result from a cat having had the terminal joint of its toes chopped off. Instead, they focus on the animal's ability to *survive* the mutilation and continue living as a household pet.

Which brings up the issue of The Doctor's Dilemma: It's probably as hard for you as for me to imagine that any reputable veterinarian actually *approves* of disabling a healthy animal. Why, then, do so many agree to it? I've never dared ask any vets I've known if they'd be willing to declaw a cat at a client's request. Yet I'm guessing that some would answer: Yes, they'll do it — but *only* if they see no alternative. Meaning, no hope of persuading the owner to continue keeping and caring for his cat — instead of euthanizing or abandoning it — if the surgery isn't performed.

A draconian choice. Is it preferable for the cat to be put to sleep or dumped? Or to survive, maimed *but alive*, as a pet in a family home?

Queen's original owners must have insisted on the last option and convinced their vet to cooperate. But then, for reasons unknown, they decided not to keep her anyway and dumped the fragile creature they'd spent so much to cripple. Sneaky, treacherous people! At least they chucked her where she'd be rescued. Then, after her year in the shelter with her handicap ignored, and her hopeful fresh start as my Angela, she had to revert to being Queen again. (The name "Angela" was thus freed for a later pet of mine.)

The same day she went back I came home with a new adoptee (next chapter). When I spoke with the shelter director a couple of weeks later, I learned that they'd belatedly made an extra effort to place Queen. She was now settled as a *wanted* indoor-only pet in what sounded like a nice, quiet home with a woman recently bereaved of her aged cat. I warmly hope this match flourished and endured. I hope too that the shelter staff have taken to heart their overdue lesson from Queen. Never again will they overlook an incoming cat's absence of claws! Never again will they fail to make special note of its vulnerability — and take prompt steps to find a welcoming home for its special needs.

· 20 ·

Molly

A Dainty Tortie

After the dismaying false start with Queen, Molly became the first bona fide member of my Fourth Generation.

From here on, my cat stories don't have endings. Starting with Molly, the rest of my pets — with one cruel, mystifying exception — are still living with me as I write. Nor have I recorded much eventful material about them to share. Yet this generation of cats might well turn out to be my last. So, as we age together, I value our relationship as much as a human family's.

Back to March 2004: Within an hour of returning Queen to the shelter, I chose a charming new pet in exchange. The staff called this cat "Willa." Small, shy and dainty, she'd been turned in the previous March as a pregnant year-old stray. They had vetted and spayed her, aborting the kittens (this is safe when done not too close to delivery). Then she'd remained there, available for adoption, an entire year. No takers — who knows why? She was certainly cute and sweet enough to appeal. A special plus in her favor, from my perspective, was *no* resemblance whatever to Daisy, whose place she was slated to fill.

Indeed, being a tortoiseshell, she resembled no other cat of mine before or since.

The coat of a tortoiseshell cat, just like a tortoiseshell comb, is a mottled or brindled mix of reddish-orange and brownish-black. Muriel Beadle, in her illuminating book *The Cat* (1977, Simon & Schuster), explains that the tweedy blend is due to the presence in the cat's sex chromosomes of pigment genes for both orange and black — an unusual color combination which occurs almost exclusively in females. If the same animal also carries a gene for white spotting, the result is what we call a calico cat, also known as a tricolor, showing distinct patches of orange, white and black.

So the "tortie," as the cat fancy has named her, is actually a variant of the calico. A different variant is a "pastel" or "rainbow" cat like my long-ago Rosalie, whose three colors emerged as a blend of pinkish-grey with white. Beadle reports that only about 6 percent of all cats are tortoiseshell or calico, and among these the ratio of females to males is 3,000 to 1. The few males are, without exception, sterile.

"Willa" was quickly rebaptized Molly. I'd been holding the name in reserve for a diminutive, very feminine pet. It also happened to be my maternal grandmother's name. I never knew her because she died when my mother was only ten, but judging from family photos she was a beauty (though overweight by today's standards). I'd describe my own four-footed Molly as more beguiling than beautiful. She has a grave, pensive little face. Her big green eyes ringed with chocolate streaks remind me of a lemur's startled gaze.

The only tribute in song to a "Molly" I've heard in recent years was a raucous blast in a movie, *King Ralph,* that went in part: "Good golly, miss Molly, sure like to ball; when you're rockin' and a rollin', can't hear your mama call…" Hardly a soundtrack fit for my demure little tortie. Going back a century or so, "sweet Molly Malone" who sold "cockles and mussels alive, alive-oh" in Dublin's fair city might be a more suitable namesake — both being partial to seafood.

Introduced to her new home, my Molly was timid to the point of passivity. The first few days she camped under beds. When I reached to pull her out her razor-sharp claws would dig fiercely into the rug she rested on until I gently disengaged each paw. (Such a contrast with the poor amputee Queen!) Before long, realizing she was among friends, she emerged from her cowering places to share space with her new family. Felicia and Freddy accepted her presence, paying little attention to her. For my part, I quickly learned that people should not reach out uninvited to touch her; instead, they must wait till *she* voluntarily chooses to approach *them*.

This diffidence is common in cats, particularly females. It's a major inconvenience only when the animal *must* be handled to be medicated, placed in a carrier for a vet visit, etc. After our loving years together, Molly trusts me enough to submit to my handling. Even so, I can approach her with ease to give her, say, her monthly squirt of Frontline during the tick season, only when she's fully relaxed — preferably snoozing.

She has bursts of affection at odd moments of her own choosing. While I'm seated in the bathroom, for example, she'll barge in and cruise lovingly around my ankles, begging — in vain! — to be gathered up for a lap-cuddle. Then there are the times I'm at work on my computer, with reference material placed neatly nearby. Molly jumps on the desk and executes a few figure-eights. She curls herself adorably on my paperwork, inviting me to rub her head and tummy. Chased off, she settles atop my printer for a nap. Perhaps, like Daisy, she was a secretary in an earlier life.

This is all typical cat behavior, most owners learn. It's part of their charm. Another fascinating quality is their sudden, unpredictable change of long-ingrained habits. For ages, Molly's favorite sleep spot was underneath the bedspread, just below the pillow, of the bed next to the guest-room window. Every morning I had to smooth and straighten the same section of the same coverlet she'd snuggled under overnight. Then, one day, she switched to the *top* of the cover on the *other* bed. I'm sure you too have known cats who adopt a favorite snoozing spot for months, even years — until one fine day their preference abruptly changes. This keeps all of us from getting bored.

Molly has been an endearing, low-key companion and an easy, low-maintenance pet. She enjoys her not-too-lengthy excursions outdoors, where she's proved a crack hunter: her trophy count of chipmunks and field mice puts her siblings to shame. Now she is middle-aged. In future she'll surely require more medical attention than just the annual checkups and booster shots she's been subjected to so far. Given her instinctive flight reflex, I'm not looking forward to the day when I need to pill her or force some other intrusive therapy on her skittish little person.

But for cat people like me, these challenges just come with the territory. We adapt without complaint because we simply can't manage *without* our companions. Even the high-maintenance ones — like my next adoptee after Molly.

21

(Authentic) Angela
Champion Couch Potato

Angela has two conspicuous distinctions. She's the laziest pet I've ever lived with, and the most allergic. Both are manageable; they don't diminish my fondness for her.

"Angela," as you learned, was what I'd called Queen — until I discovered the poor creature was declawed and gave her back to the shelter. Then, a year and a half later, I revived and reassigned the name. It nicely suited the plump, sweet-faced cat who filled the vacancy left by Felicia's death a few months earlier.

My new, authentic Angela was the same age as Molly. In fact she'd been available at the same shelter in March 2004 when I went there to look for a new pet four months after losing Daisy. But at that point I didn't seriously consider adopting her because her coloring — grey markings on white — reminded me too much of Daisy. So instead, after my misstep with Queen, I chose the tortoiseshell.

By September 2005, however — a year and a half later — I was mourning the loss of Felicia, my grey tabby. This time I disregarded any candidates resembling *her*. So buxom, gentle Angela now looked appealing as a sister for youthful Molly and middle-aged Freddy.

She had been turned in to the shelter by a rescue group as a pregnant stray, estimated age one year, in April 2003. She was thoroughly tame, so must have started life near people in some kind of home environment. As with Molly, her kittens were aborted during spay surgery. Then she spent the *next two and a half years* awaiting adoption in the cat kennel. Not once in all that time did anyone offer her a home! Her skin ailment may have been a major deterrent; more about this in a moment.

As her months in the shelter dragged on, Angela's sedentary lifestyle and self-feeding of the dry kibble always on hand encouraged her heft, flab and apathetic temperament. Still — she had a pretty face and was sweet-natured and easygoing. She was obviously well adapted to living with other cats. And after her long dreary incarceration, she certainly deserved a break. So I gathered her up and brought her home, allergies and all.

Years earlier I'd gained some experience with allergic cats. Both Tim and Lucky, you may recall, suffered severe skin reactions to flea bites. But once I succeeded in protecting those pets against fleas (adults, larvae and eggs) with medicated collars and household pesticides, they had no further dermatitis problem. Angela's sensitivity, however, was far more generalized — and acute. She constantly itched and scratched, compulsively licked and chewed her coat. She shed excessively for a shorthaired cat, biting off little chunks of fur, raising nasty lesions and scabs over much of her body.

No specific cause had been identified. The shelter's veterinarians had given her several injections of methylprednisolone (marketed as Depo-Medrol). Each time this anti-inflammatory drug alleviated her symptoms for several weeks — but failed to eliminate whatever allergen(s) provoked them. Moreover, repeated doses of powerful medications like corticosteroids to relieve discomfort can have dangerous side effects, such as high risk of diabetes.

I immediately took Angela to my own vet. His tests confirmed a diagnosis of allergy, rather than infection, as the basic irritant. He prescribed a daily diet supplement of salmon oil (rich in omega-3 fatty acids) to strengthen her immune system and antihistamine pills to soothe her sensitivity. I followed this regimen for the next few months, during which the doctor also gave her one Depo-Medrol injection. All helped her feel and look better. But long term, we needed to deal with the root cause. Angela was still a young cat. Ideally she would enjoy many good years ahead *if* her allergens could be identified, managed and subdued — even if not wholly eradicated.

As a first step, my doctor referred me to a veterinary dermatologist he knew and respected. A *long* car ride, to the same distant specialist practice where Daisy's ophthalmologist had treated her a few years earlier. Angela's consultation visit did not go well. Due to a scheduling switch which no one bothered to notify me of before I left home, she was examined by a substitute doctor for the dermatologist I'd made the appointment with. This unsatisfactory replacement lectured me with boilerplate about pet allergies. She urged me, as one piece of poor advice, to use Advantage flea treatment. (Never mind that Advantage is useless against ticks, which infest my rural community, whereas the parasite product I've long used, Frontline, is effective against *both* ticks and fleas.) She checked Angela for ringworm and mites (needlessly; my vet had already done that). Then, to test for food allergies, the dermatologist recommended a 12-week-long trial of proteins to which Angela was unaccustomed: perhaps home-cooked meals, or a special prescription diet based on rabbit, peas and other foods that cats don't normally eat.

This idea *I* ruled out on the spot. Even if the trial did identify foods to avoid because they irritate the skin, I couldn't envisage forcing just one of my pets to stick indefinitely to her own, exclusive hypoallergenic diet. (That would be even more of an ordeal than keeping one declawed cat inside the house while letting the other cats in and out freely.) No! I was willing to try some *relatively* hypoallergenic new commercial foods, top quality and nutritionally balanced, that *all* my cats could benefit from together. But Angela — who dearly loves to eat — would never be forced to subsist on a separate, customized menu for the rest of her life.

After this useless outing I conferred with my primary vet, who in turn spoke to the dermatologist I'd originally been meant to see. Having decided not to subject Angela to any drastic diet changes, we agreed to pursue investigation of the other major culprit: *airborne* allergens. These include a long list of tree pollens, molds, dust mites, insects and other offenders circulating in the environment.

A blood test exists to identify specific airborne substances to which a given animal is allergic. Then, a custom vaccine can be formulated with antigens for that animal's particular sensitivities. A course of immunization therapy (called "aqueous hyposensitization") is begun. The made-to-order serum is injected under the skin at regular intervals, starting with small frequent doses and gradually progressing to larger amounts given farther apart — a long-term maintenance program. (This is similar in principle to the immunotherapy which desensitizes people allergic to cat dander. You may recall it was administered to my sneezing friend Karen, mentioned earlier.) According to the laboratory in Pasadena, California which developed the special vaccine for Angela, "hyposensitization therapy is effective in approximately 75%-80% of atopic dogs and cats [those with inborn allergies]" — but "the majority of cases will require lifelong allergy shots at a 14- to 20-day interval."

I gave Angela her first shot on June 21, 2006, nine months after her adoption. Over the following weeks the volume and frequency of her dose were carefully regulated until, after four months, we'd progressed to the "maintenance" level: one milliliter of serum injected every three weeks. Once the initial, intensive period of adaptation was past, the process became easy. A vial of desensitizing serum is stored in my refrigerator. The cost isn't onerous: currently $17 per dose (less than $300 a year). Angela submits without protest to the needle jabs spaced 21 days apart. If I'm away on the scheduled date, a pet sitter administers her shot from my written instructions.

Her only serious relapse occurred in early fall 2010, four years after the treatment began. Instead of re-testing her blood, the allergist in California recommended diluting the existing serum and re-starting the desensitization process from scratch. This worked! By the following spring she was back on track, with a huge improvement in the condition of her skin and quality of her fur coat. She — and her sibling cats — have also benefited from some premium dry foods that contain few or no allergenic ingredients like corn.

To this day Angela continues on the same regimen; I expect her to remain indefinitely on immunization therapy. At some point she may need to have her blood retested and her medication formula adjusted. But her response thus far justifies the whole ongoing treatment as worthwhile.

By nature, I've never been a perfectionist — fortunately! since this spares me constant disappointment in life. *Improvement,* rather than total achievement, is my normal goal when attacking tasks and problems. An outcome that is strikingly *better,* even if not ideal, usually satisfies me — particularly if the ideal result entails an unreasonable investment of time and effort, a disruptive change of routine, or a risky gamble. So Angela's very visible improvement has made me very happy!

Apart from her serum shots, Angela's skin needs one other safeguard. One freezing day in midwinter I noticed bite marks and flea residue on her fur. Normally, in the cold season when fleas and ticks can't survive outdoors, I suspend the cats' monthly pest-control treatments. But apparently enough fleas and flea eggs had been overwintering in the warm house, hidden in rugs and upholstery, to infest and irritate Angela. She, like Tim and Lucky years earlier, obviously needed *year-round* flea protection, indoors as well as out. An immediate dose of Frontline cleared her up.

Another, minor health problem has been an occasional wheezing cough. The vet thinks this could be a mild case of bronchial asthma related to her allergic weakness. Once, when she went off her food but showed no other symptoms of infection, he effectively treated her with bronchodilator pills. She also tends to be constipated. So I switched to a dry food formula with higher fiber content ("hairball control" claims the package label), which can't help but benefit all the cats.

As noted at the outset, I find Angela's face quite pretty. But she has a terrible figure! Though she may have a *tendency* to obesity, I never pander to her gluttonous appetite. She's not measurably overweight, staying within the normal 10-to-12-pound range for an adult shorthaired spayed female. But her huge soft belly spreads far too wide and loose, nearly dragging the floor as she walks. She resembles those perpetual mother cats swollen from dropping litter after litter.

How did she develop that ponderous, swaying abdomen? Obviously, two and a half years of idle lounging in the animal shelter didn't help. Her athletic activity there must have been confined to batting an occasional toy, swiping a scratching post, rearranging herself from position A to position B for her next nap — *and* making frequent forays to the dish with unlimited kibble to nibble.

But then why weren't her long-term shelter mates flabby too? Molly, for one, had been immobilized there an entire year, yet had a trim, compact little body when I met her — and still does. More to the point now, why didn't Angela manage to work off much of her blubber *after* she moved in with me? Beyond her first weeks of settling into the house, she was free nearly every day to wander, run, chase, climb and explore outdoors as much as she liked.

Sorry to say, there's a simple answer: *Angela is incorrigibly lazy.* The epithet "couch potato" could well have been coined for her. She abhors and avoids exercise. Is her lethargy a genetic trait? A quirk of temperament? The result of early illness or trauma? A symptom of her allergic vulnerability? Whatever the reason, there seems no remedy. She's been thoroughly checked by her vet. Apart from the allergy and sluggish intestine, her general health is good.

Whereas the typical house cat sleeps 75 percent of the day, Angela spends closer to 90 percent of her time snoozing. She even naps outdoors. Her preferred hour to venture out is twilight — predator instinct for the crepuscular hunt! — but she doesn't choose to stay outside long or travel far. Though I've disposed of a few dead field mice in places near the house where Angela likes to hang out, I haven't seen her actually pursue prey or make a kill. Now and then she'll pounce on a swooping moth or blowing leaf or, indoors, wrestle with a catnip toy. In her years with me she's become *slightly* more mobile. But she remains unchallenged champion of one activity: curled up dozing on a soft piece of furniture.

There *is* an upside to her sluggish disposition. Angela is the most even-tempered cat I've ever known. Here she outshines even laid-back Felicia and Toby, both models of equanimity and adaptability. Unlike most felines, Angela's calm isn't shattered by sudden loud noises, or large strange men tramping through her space, or unfamiliar animals and machines near her turf. (One time as I drove out of my garage, honking at Angela to get out of the way, she kept sitting passively in the path of the car until I literally had to chase her off.) She's not the least bit shy with people. She doesn't voluntarily approach visitors to make friends, as Toby and Freddy used to. But she responds to their petting with purrs and relaxes near the social group in her serene, decorative way.

Angela has just one horrendous habit: exercising her claws on my prized hand-hooked living room rug. It drives me crazy; after all, she has two top-quality sisal scratching posts at her disposal. (Yes, she uses them too!) But I've learned I can't "train" her to spare my treasured rug and must shriek at her every time she attacks it.

Like Rosalie years ago, Angela can be a closet queen. She enjoys retreating for a private snooze on the fresh towels in the dark quiet depths of the linen closet. Luckily, she can't close the door behind her to become trapped and forgotten in there.

She and her cat siblings get along fine, though there's little one-on-one interaction. With me, she's trusting and confident. She submits placidly to my handling: serum injections, brushing, combing, occasional pilling. She spends part of many nights on my bed, rousing me now and then with little murmurs, whines and sighs as she sleeps. This "talking" in her cat dreams is quickly quieted by my hand reaching over to stroke her. Her most ardent moments — the *only* times she approaches me purely for love — are evenings while I'm watching TV. She jumps in my lap, nuzzles and licks my face passionately for a few moments, then settles her soft bulk nearby for the next nap. She's obviously driven by affection, not appetite, since we've all long finished dinner.

Actually, despite her allergy, Angela isn't such a high-maintenance pet after all. Her few special needs are really quite simple to care for. She's not too bright and I can't say I find her behavior interesting. But in her languid, undemanding way she can be a sweet and satisfying companion.

22

Charlie

An Inexplicable Loss

For those who allow outdoor freedom to their cats it's an all-too-common calamity: Suddenly, one day, a pet just disappears. Without a trace or a clue. (In most cases, but not all, it wore no identification.) Never again is the animal seen or heard of, alive or dead. The family never learns what happened or why.

Heartbreaking, you'll agree. But not so hard to anticipate — given the risks we knowingly take whenever we permit our pets to run loose.

Well, it took all of 32 years and 16 indoor-outdoor pets before *this* permissive owner suffered *this* particular calamity. Was I lucky to be spared that long? I can hear the smug I-told-you-so's from lobbyists for an indoor-only policy. (And how self-righteously they'd harrumph if they knew, too, that four of my earlier cats had been killed by cars.) Whether or not I should feel guilt for this latest, inexplicable loss, I was devastated.

Little Charlie was a dear, delightful pet. He was already proving a worthy successor to my adored Freddy. Our attachment deepened and a new Special Relationship was developing. But our time together turned out to be pitifully brief: a mere eight months.

By September 2006, I'd recovered enough from the blow of Freddy's death four months earlier to seek a new little brother for Molly and Angela. (Freddy had actually been a big brother — their senior by seven years.) As I set out for the shelter, what I more or less had in mind was an adolescent/young adult, between one and three years old, whose color and markings would never remind me of Freddy.

What immediately riveted my eye, however, as I walked into the cat quarters was an adorable *kitten* in a cage by himself. Coincidentally he was just the same age, five months, as Freddy had been when I adopted him from the veterinary hospital. But happily, there was no resemblance at all to Freddy's vanilla-butterscotch coloring. *This* little fellow was sleekest black with a few spanking white accents: whiskers, mittens, ankle socks, a streak from chin on down through his underside.

Instant enchantment! The staff called him "Billie". He'd been brought there with his (tame) mother and several littermates in May. They'd all been fostered in a private home for a couple of months before being admitted to the shelter proper for adoption.

"Billie" had to be housed separately because of a persistent upper-respiratory infection. But his cold didn't inhibit him from being warmly responsive when I gathered him up for a get-acquainted hug. The staff told me he'd been handled and cuddled a lot and was engagingly friendly with everyone. No socializing needed here!

I dutifully toured the cat rooms and looked at the many young candidates waiting for homes; shelters are always filled to capacity at summer's end. But I kept coming back to the ebony kitten with his snowy whiskers and paws and gleaming gold eyes. Finally, I told the executive director that "Billie" was my first choice. If his respiratory ailment wasn't contagious or difficult to treat, I'd take him as soon as they were willing to release him.

They agreed to put a temporary hold on him for me. His medical condition was then reviewed jointly, via fax and phone, by the shelter's veterinarians and my own. The doctors' consensus: though "Billie" might require antibiotics a few times a year, his respiratory problem wouldn't affect my other cats and there was no reason he couldn't be adopted. So, a couple of days later, I went to fetch him home.

I quickly rebaptized him Charlie, a name I'd always liked. It was also a tribute to a veterinarian (by then retired) who had taken wonderful care of my pets for nearly 20 years. No time was lost having Charlie thoroughly checked over by my present vet. As matters turned out, he acquired a good-sized medical dossier over the next months.

First, there was his recurring respiratory infection. It involved sneezing, a nasal discharge, lethargy and appetite loss but no fever; each episode was successfully treated with an antibiotic called Zithromax. Then, quite separately, there was frequent tearing from his right eye. At first my doctor thought it was due to a condition called follicular conjunctivitis. This wasn't serious, he assured me, and could be treated with anti-inflammatory drops if it didn't clear up by itself. But further tests revealed the cause to be a blocked tear duct. Various ophthalmic medications were tried without success. Finally, Charlie had surgery under anesthesia to flush out the tear duct. However, the blockage, from mucus or some other agent, was found to be so solid that it could *not* be perforated during the procedure. So Charlie would just have to continue living with his leaking eye — unless the ophthalmologist who had treated Daisy's eye problems could find a solution. Alas, Charlie didn't remain with me long enough for a consultation visit to this specialist.

The third item in Charlie's veterinary dossier was a slight heart murmur. I mentioned earlier that this same symptom — an abnormal sound heard with the stethoscope — had been detected during Freddy's annual exams over the years:. So now, still jolted by the shock of Freddy's unexplained demise, I determined to explore Charlie's heart condition early and exhaustively. At my request, an internist who does ultrasound diagnostic tests performed an echocardiogram on Charlie — more revealing than a simple chest X-ray. His report: "mild left ventricular dilation" but "no identifiable insufficiencies, masses or effusions." His recommendation: although no cardiac medication was needed "at this time," the dilation of the left heart chamber should be rechecked by repeating the echo test in nine months. In other words, explained my primary veterinarian, all we need do now is keep a careful eye on the situation.

All this medical attention to a brand-new pet, not yet a year old, was costing a pretty penny. My veterinary file shows that in one month, April, I spent nearly $750 on my kitten's eye and heart conditions. But Charlie was worth it! Overall he thrived. When his appetite wasn't crimped by a cold he ate voraciously. He steadily filled out and grew into a handsome teenager. He had a beautiful nature, too. As I described him in a note to a sitter, "… lively, bright, warm, affectionate, playful, energetic — the most people-oriented of the three [cats]. Loves to be cuddled. He still needs to be taught nice manners and proper behavior, but is quick to learn and aims to please."

Charlie's not-so-nice manners were on display when he lunged greedily at his sisters' food — after he'd wolfed down his own meal but they hadn't yet finished eating. But he was responding to my patient correction and adapting easily to the routines of life in his new home. He got along nicely with his sibling cats and attached himself ebulliently to his adoptive mom. Outdoors, he quickly learned his way around our immediate neighborhood. I watched him exploring and playing happily in the garden, woods and hedgerow. Presumably he stayed within earshot because — if he hadn't already come home on his own — he always answered my dinner call promptly.

Always, that is, until May 29, 2007. I won't forget that date!

That Tuesday was a brilliant spring morning. The Memorial Day weekend was over and two painters had arrived to do some touchup work outdoors. I let the three cats out, as usual, after their breakfast. From the kitchen window I could see Charlie and Angela heading together across the driveway. Both peered curiously at the painters' parked truck as they trotted past it into the adjoining woods. Angela soon came home again for one of her couch-potato snoozes. Charlie didn't reappear all day.

By dinnertime, when he failed to respond to my summons, I worried a bit. First time my gluttonous little boy had been late for a meal! Throughout the evening I repeatedly whistled and clapped and called for him. In vain. When I finally went to bed that night I half expected — remembering earlier episodes with no-show cats — to see him back home first thing in the morning. But no. And then no. And no again!

After two entire days and nights Charlie still hadn't shown up and nobody had called to report finding him. (He was, of course, wearing an ID tag engraved with my phone number.) So I launched a systematic search. I did everything I'd done when Felicia vanished eight years earlier — and more. I printed up a MISSING CAT flyer with Charlie's photo for display on neighborhood utility poles, the pet-supply shop, three local veterinary hospitals and community bulletin boards in local stores. I registered his information with lost-and-found-pet services at a local radio station, the town's Animal Control office, and a nearby private animal shelter (not the same one my own pets were adopted from). I checked that when the town's Highway Department crews pick up road-killed dogs and cats, they notify the owners of any pets with identification.

Then, I conducted a house-by-house canvass. I rang doorbells or phoned all my immediate neighbors. I either showed them Charlie's photo or left my missing-cat flyer in their mailbox. If no one was home I snooped shamelessly around the premises. I peered into sheds and dumpsters, garages and wells and basement crawl spaces where a curious young cat might get trapped while exploring. One unoccupied house with a broker's For Sale sign had a swimming pool out back, brimful with water but no protective fence. Apprehensively, I inspected the pool bottom; thankfully, no drowned victims were visible. Even so, because the unguarded pool posed a danger to wandering children and wildlife as well as pets, I reported the safety violation to the town building code office.

Not least, I forced myself on a slow, painstaking patrol along all the nearby streets. I'd never seen Charlie venture onto the road; mercifully, he acted scared of cars. But suppose that Tuesday he'd been pursuing (or pursued by) something that drove him heedlessly into the street? If he'd been hit, then managed to stagger away and collapse somewhere off-road, no highway employee or passing Good Samaritan would have noticed him. So I peered into all the bordering woods, hedgerows, tall grass and tangled brush for any sign of his little dark shape. Nothing!

By his second week missing my spirits darkened. I began to lose hope. An animal can survive quite a while without food but will die of thirst after a few days with no water. Here, barely a year after Freddy deserted me, had I lost a new little love? *Not knowing what happened* was the worst part. Several pet owners I know have suffered the mystery disappearance of an animal — usually one with no visible ID. But Charlie had left home wearing his conspicuous red collar and stainless-steel name tag. (He'd also been microchipped at adoption. But only a veterinary or shelter facility with a scanner can read the chip to trace a pet's owner; neighbors are of no help here.) For me, then, this first unexplained loss was as bewildering as it was devastating.

With suggestions from friends, I compiled some speculative scenarios for *why* Charlie vanished into thin air.

One possibility could be ruled out immediately: voluntary absence. Knowing Charlie, I'm absolutely certain he didn't choose to run away, walk about, or spend a holiday in someone else's home. He'd become too attached to his cozy territory, his tasty menus, his adoring owner, his two amiable cat siblings. No — he was *prevented* from coming back.

I'm also convinced that whatever did prevent him occurred before dark. With the summer solstice just three weeks away, we still had daylight long past the dinner hour I'd been calling Charlie home for, in vain. So, nocturnal threats like blinding head-lights, feral attack cats, predatory raccoons, foxes or great horned owls seemed pretty much ruled out. Daytime hunters like coy-otes, who prey on pet cats, are mercifully absent from our region. As for the occasional pack of aggressive dogs, if they're not chased away by local homeowners, their target cat can escape up a tree.

Sudden fatal illness? *If* Charlie had been an elderly, enfeebled cat — as weak as Toby had become toward the end — he might have succumbed to a stroke or heart attack in some out-of-the-way nook. (When cats sense they're dying, they retreat to a hiding place. I'd already witnessed this twice at home: terminally ill Jenny concealing herself in a closet; Freddy burrowing beneath a bed.) But one-year-old Charlie, neutered and vaccinated, afflicted with nothing worse than a runny nose and a leaking eye, was much too hale and hearty to suffer geriatric collapse.

A more likely fate would have been *progressive* weakening and eventual death from becoming trapped and deprived of air and/or water. Had he fallen into into an unused cellar, or a smoth-ering pile of mulch, or a vat of paint, or a dumpster to be hauled to the landfill? Did he jump into a passing delivery truck? Stow away in the vehicle of a construction worker who commutes to his local job from many miles away? If Charlie was accidentally carted off to a distant community, how come nobody at that end noticed the little ID tag dangling from his neck and phoned to notify me? We've all heard those believe-it-or-not tales of a pet (usually a dog) which, after weeks or months missing, turns up in some outlandishly faraway spot or — most mind-boggling — manages to find its own way home. I couldn't dismiss any sce-nario! But I pinned few hopes on Charlie's reappearance beyond our immediate neighborhood.

My pet-sitter friends Ann and Phil wondered if Charlie might have been kidnapped. Not for ransom but because, they wrote me, "he was so friendly, so easy to know and love." But, I protested, what about his ID? *Who* would deliberately keep an animal clearly labeled as someone's pet?

Well, two theories. Charlie's collar could conceivably have come off. Though I'm scrupulous to the point of fanaticism about equipping pets with tagged collars, I have to admit that their *visible* ID is less dependably permanent than the invisible microchips. (That's why the belt-and-suspenders system, using *both* a tag and a chip, is sensible insurance.) As it happened, Charlie had managed to slough off his buckled leather collar on my lawn a few weeks earlier. So the day he went missing he was sporting a fresh braided-nylon collar, snug-fitting, with a secure snap fastener. But because it was slightly elasticized, the possibility of yanking it off couldn't be entirely excluded.

Second theory: Whoever kidnapped Charlie for adoption intentionally removed, or chose to disregard, his identification. The most lurid script of all!. It conjures a picture of some dotty, lonely crone enticing my Charlie — eager, friendly, trusting — into her miserable lair to imprison as a trophy pet. Must he remain the witch's captive for life? Could he ever escape to come home on his own? Would she one day relent, or tire of caring for him, enough to set him free?

Realistically, though, as the months went by, I learned to live with a more plausible answer to Charlie's absence. I guessed that he'd been hit by a car. Then, he managed to crawl off and succumb in some deep brush far from anyone's notice — including my own roadside inspection tour. All I can hope is that his suffering was brief.

Miracles can't be excluded, of course. If by some incredible chance Charlie ever does reappear, I'll always have a welcoming place for him. Today, I just treasure the memory of the short time spent with this loving, captivating young cat.

What did I learn from the experience?

One lesson is a challenge to one of my firm principles. Charlie's conspicuous identification turned out to be no help whatever in locating my lost pet, alive or dead. Indeed, thinking back, the only two times ID *did* succeed in reuniting me with missing cats was when they were dead. You'll remember that Harry and Toby, both roadkilled, were each found by people who kindly took the trouble to examine their tagged collars.

Nonetheless, my faith in the value of having *all* pets wear legible ID at *all* times hasn't flagged. On several occasions I've phoned neighbors whose tagged dogs wandered onto my premises. The worried owners were grateful to learn where their pets were and come fetch them home. Even without *reading* the ID on one of my free-roaming cats, anyone in the area can instantly recognize it as an owned pet, not to be mistaken for a stray.

The other lesson from the cruel loss of Charlie: Here's one more example to reinforce the warnings against letting our cats run loose outdoors — even in perfect weather, brilliant daylight, a tranquil neighborhood. Yes, our pets always court danger. Yes, they always risk tragedy. And *we* gamble with their safety and health and survival each time we open our doors to set them at liberty.

Yet I, for one, vote once more to continue running those risks. At heart I'm still convinced that *quality* of life for an indoor-outdoor cat counts more than longevity.

23

Alex

The New Little Man

Four months after Charlie vanished, his successor joined the household.

This bereavement period gave me and the surviving cats ample time to adjust to his absence (if not to the enduring pain of the unanswerable "Why?"). As with the earlier departures of Felicia and then Freddy, who both also died in May, the mourning interval tided us over the hectic summer season. By early fall, when

I came back from an overseas trip, the pace was slower and my schedule more settled. *Now* was the moment to fill the vacancy in home and heart by welcoming a new pet who needed a family into ours.

As always in September, shelters were chock-a-block with cats and kittens. Arriving at my customary source to look over the candidates, I had one firm precondition: *no* resemblance to Charlie! I also felt a boy would be more readily accepted by Molly and Angela.

One young male was particularly striking. He was as snow-white as Charlie had been jet-black. Well, *almost* all white. I detected a few pale hints of peach on his ears, tail and back. Coincidentally, this little fellow was the same age, between four and five months, that Charlie had been when adopted exactly one year earlier — and that Freddy had been when adopted in September a dozen years before. All from the bumper crop of kittens harvested every spring without fail.

The shelter staff had dubbed the white kitten "Peter." He'd been rescued in late May (just when Charlie vanished), age about three weeks, together with two littermates. No mother cat was found. The tiny trio was fostered privately in a volunteer's home for a few months, then admitted to the public facility. "Peter"'s two brothers — one black and white, one orange and white — had already been adopted by the time I met him. Their parents must have been a colorful mix.

Add to his pristine whiteness other striking features: vivid blue eyes; a delicate pointed face; a slender fine-boned body; a spectacularly long and sinuous tail tinted with faint rings of pinkish-orange. Sitting upright in patrician pose, he reminded me of an Egyptian cat god's statuette perched on a museum pedestal. He was so fascinating to look at, and friendly to boot, that I saw no need to prolong the search. "Peter" was processed for adoption and brought home that very day.

What permanent name would best suit him?

Reviewing symbolic possibilities, I dismissed Frosty, Snowball, Sugar, Icecap and other color-cued banalities. Of the "real" male names I liked — Roy, Michael, Jeff, Edward, Philip, Andrew, Roger and a few others — none seemed to *connect* with this little guy's demeanor. I certainly wouldn't inflict an Egyptian god's name on him. (I think their cat deity was a god*dess*, in any case.) So I sought an aristocratic analogy elsewhere.

What soon sprang to mind was the image of a White Russian nobleman — lean, elegant, brilliant blue eyes in the dazzling snowscape of Siberia. *Da!* My new pet would share the name of a czar — the *good* czar Alexander II, the ruler who freed Russia's serfs even before Lincoln freed America's slaves. Thus my little prince was christened to reign as Alex.

The most noteworthy feature of his first year with me, in terms of what I learned and spent, was — believe it or not — his digestive tract. Here, let me insert a sidebar on a topic unmentioned so far: how I feed my cats.

From the time I adopted Lucy and Rosalie over three decades ago, I've adhered pretty faithfully to the same system. My pets are served two meals a day. Whatever they don't finish is removed. No food is left out in the dishes for round-the-clock self-feeding! No fat cats appreciated here! Only on the rare evenings I go out very early and expect to come home late do I leave a little kibble in the bowls to tide them over.

Their diet is partly canned ("wet") food, partly nuggets of dry kibble. Ideal proportions are 50-50 — wet breakfast, dry dinner. In practice, though, the mix depends on how many cats happen to be in residence and how hungry they are.

For example, for three cats — my census most of the time —
I divide the contents of a 5.5-ounce can of wet food among their
three dishes at breakfast. Anything left uneaten is stored in the
fridge and then added, warmed with tap water, to their evening
meal, which is normally a level serving spoon of dry food. If only
two cats are on hand, each gets one-third of the morning's can;
the remaining third is saved to juice up their kibble *every* night.

Which foods do I buy? All from leading pet food manufacturers, formulated for cats only and meeting the standards for
"complete and balanced nutrition" set by the Association of
American Feed Control Officials (AAFCO). I purchase canned
food at the supermarket, sticking to major national brands and
shunning the cheaper "house" labels carried by some grocery
chains.

My cats' dry food, on the other hand, is always one of the
"premium" products sold in specialty pet stores. I started buying
these years ago after a couple of pets suffered urinary problems
and their vets recommended food with a *low magnesium* content.
Such formulas were then available only in the costlier dry specialty diets. Though some mass-marketed brands have since been
improved, I still rely on the premium labels. Presently I alternate
between Hills' Science Diet and the Wellness brand — the latter
a corn-free formula that *might* be helpful for Angela's allergies. A
new pet less than a year old (Freddy, Charlie and Alex when
adopted) is initially fed the "kitten" or "growth" dry formula and
graduates to the adult product at twelve months of age.

Dry cat food, you've probably noticed, isn't available in a wide
choice of flavors. While I vary the taste as much as possible with
each new bag of kibble (chicken this time, fish the next), the *real*
variety comes in my pets' canned meals. From day one I decided
never to let them get hooked on just one or two favorite foods, so

that they'd turn up their little pink noses at everything else. (You've probably met, as I have, the pampering cat owner who claims she buys mostly Fancy Feast Turkey, or Nine Lives Tuna, or whatever, because that's what her pet "really loves." Does she also feed her child mostly fudge sundaes or French fries for the same reason?)

Early on I adopted a simple rotation system: open a can of red meat today, then poultry tomorrow, then seafood the next day. Repeat the cycle. Then, finish the week on the seventh day with one of the potluck mixes — with some indeterminate name like Gourmet Delight and, usually, "meat by-products" listed as the main ingredient on the label.

With two or three major brands and a large range of canned meats to choose among — beef, lamb, veal, liver, turkey, chicken, salmon, whitefish, tuna, shrimp, cod, etc., not to mention the extra taste when cheese or eggs or rice are added — I offer my carnivores a distinctly different flavor every morning. Naturally, each cat has personal preferences. But all are accustomed to a smorgasbord spread over the course of a week. All have learned that their food is provided in a home, not a restaurant. If the *plat du jour* isn't to a pet's liking, he or she can't select some other dish from a menu. He just must nibble enough to take the edge off his appetite and then wait till the next meal — by which time he's sure to eat more heartily.

Nowadays petite Molly is my pickiest (and slowest) eater. But there are no spoiled prima donnas in this household. Even the fussiest pets haven't trained me to pander to their tastes. Attempts at emotional blackmail — the plaintive whimper, the beseeching gaze, the sniff followed by flat refusal to touch the food, even the contemptuous covering-up motions — fail to rend my heart or yield an alternative entrée from my cupboard.

Of course I make an exception about catering to food preferences if a cat is ill. The importance of keeping the patient as fully nourished as possible always trumps the menu regimen. Inducing fragile little Harry to *just eat!* was a worrisome challenge every time his ailing liver or some other problem flared up. I'll never forget the evening he slowly ingested, bit by tiny bit, the entire pork chop I'd just cooked for my own dinner — to my immeasurable joy and relief. I've also served baby-food formulas (puréed meat with no onion powder), recommended for sick cats as highly palatable and digestible, as well as prescription diet products obtainable only from the vet's office.

What about offering "people food" to healthy cats? I rarely do this, though I don't object to giving a small extra treat *after* a proper meal of AAFCO's "complete and balanced" cat ration has been consumed. It was Toby, I recall, who adored cut-up pieces of fatty meat trimmed from my dinner steak; others would eagerly lap up any leftover melted cheese or gravy. But my current pets aren't much tempted by my leftovers. Their only regular fresh treat, every few weeks, is the raw liver and heart of a free-range chicken purchased from my neighborhood poultry farm. (The same family farm that temporarily contributed Chico/Spike to my cat household.) Finely chopped and added to their dinner kibble, the nutritious bonus is devoured with gusto.

Let's get back to Alex and *his* food history

Soon after he arrived, I became aware of something not quite right in my new kitten's eating habits. He was just the same age and size as Charlie had been when adopted a year earlier. So I expected him, like Charlie, to have the voracious appetite of a Growing Boy. Once again, I readily served hefty portions — pretty much all he wanted to eat — and watched him wolf his meals down as eagerly as Charlie had. But two things were odd.

First, Alex's defecation didn't appear normal. (During his first few weeks, while he was kept wholly indoors, I was able to monitor all his excretions in the litter boxes.) His stool, which he often deposited twice a day and never bothered to cover, tended to be loose and voluminous, pale in color, with a pungent odor. Sometimes a bout of diarrhea would follow several hours later.

Second, despite the copious quantity of food he ingested each day, Alex didn't appear to be gaining weight. His build was rangy but his torso stayed very lean. Charlie, by contrast, had become sturdy and solid as he gradually filled out on the same generous diet.

Unavoidable conclusion: my little prince wasn't getting enough nourishment! All that food he consumed was pouring through his gastrointestinal tract like a sieve. He wasn't *absorbing* enough nutrients to support healthy growth.

Medical investigation was called for. Fecal specimens were tested before the end of Alex's first month here. The result was disheartening. My new pet, reported the doctor, was afflicted with a condition known as exocrine pancreatic insufficiency, also called "maldigestion syndrome." This means that certain glands in his pancreas weren't producing the enzymes required to digest his food properly. The condition is seen more often in dogs (frequently of genetic origin) than in cats (commonly caused by chronic inflammation of the pancreas). Though incurable, it can be treated by adding an oral enzyme supplement to the pet's diet — permanently.

Oddly, this wasn't my first experience with the problem.

Thirteen years earlier, you may recall, I'd observed similar symptoms while Chico/Spike, my temporary farm cat, was staying here. Chico, unlike Alex, was a fully grown adult; nor did he look underweight. But he too had an enormous appetite, ate voluminously — and then excreted most of his food. He too was tested and found deficient in pancreatic enzymes. The vet I was using at the time prescribed an additive in powder form. Chico absolutely hated the taste of this and boycotted the food I mixed it with. So we switched him to smaller quantities of a weaker product. He seemed to tolerate this better — but then soon afterwards moved back to his farm home. There, he was given no further treatments. Yet he survived for many years. That seemed to confirm both the original verdict on his condition, "borderline," and the fact that pancreatic enzyme insufficiency, while burdensome, is *not* a life-threatening affliction.

Recalling Chico, I shuddered at the idea of inflicting on little Alex the unending ordeal of a diet supplement from the very start of his life here. But what choice did I have? I purchased an initial supply of the enzyme powder prescribed by my current vet. Alex, just like Chico, couldn't abide the taste and refused to eat. I made inquiries online about alternatives. The enzyme was also produced in pill form; should I try substituting this for the powder? No, replied one expert, tablets dissolve less effectively in the pet's stomach. Instead, she advised mixing the powder in some broth and administering it as an oral liquid. To try this twice a day, *every* day, struck me as impractical.

So after a few days I gave up. I returned the unused enzyme powder (exorbitantly expensive!) to the clinic for credit. Meanwhile, they gave Alex some added tests. A complete blood chemistry analysis showed his kidneys, liver, blood sugar, etc. to all be normal. Good news!

Even better news emerged from a separate blood test known as TLI (for "trypsin-like immunoreactivity") which measures pancreatic enzyme sufficiency. The blood serum is sent to a specialized lab for feline TLI analysis and provides a much more accurate determination than a fecal specimen can. Here, to my happy surprise, the finding was "normal" too. In retrospect, my vet explained, Alex's initial and less reliable fecal test had yielded a "false positive" result.

At the same time, Alex's elimination pattern was improving. I observed fewer instances of unnaturally copious, loose stool and diarrhea. (It's possible I missed some, because he was by now spending part of the day outdoors with access to Mother Nature's own vast litter box.) Moreover, I was no longer feeding him as much as he wanted to eat. Overloading his digestive tract may, in fact, have helped provoke the excessive pooping. So I now added just a *little* extra kibble to his regular meal portions. Gradually, too, he was gaining weight. After four months here he'd attained 8.8 pounds, which the doctor pronounced "good" for his age of 8½ months.

The following month Alex underwent a thyroid test, X-rays, and an ultrasound exam. Results: normal thyroid; a mildly enlarged heart with no evidence of impaired function; and mild enlargement of the lymph nodes. This last suggested possible enteritis (intestinal inflammation). Treatment with the antibiotic metronidazole (brand name Flagyl) was recommended, so Alex consumed these tiny pills twice a day in his food for a few weeks. He continued to fill out and eliminate more normally.

By now, my energetic little man with his erratic digestion had been pretty thoroughly vetted. Yet there was one more exploratory option I'd been holding in reserve: an endoscopic exam by a gastroenterologist. This would be the same specialist who had treated Jenny's stomach cancer 15 years earlier. By the time I finally took Alex there for consultation, my patient was a year old. He looked and acted healthy; his frame was slender rather than scrawny, the stool in his intestines felt normally firm when the doctor palpated. His "insatiable" appetite was not a cause for worry, I was assured, since he seemed to be *using* most of the nutrients he was ingesting. I could continue feeding him generously — though not so heavily as to make him sick. "At this point," concluded the specialist, my pet's general condition didn't justify the stress and expense of an endoscopy — an invasive procedure performed under anesthesia. We left it that I'd get in touch with the gastroenterologist again if any new or repeated problems ever arose.

What a relief!

Since then, Alex has been fine. One year after his adoption, when given a checkup and booster shots by his primary vet, he weighed nearly 12 pounds. No longer lean but svelte, my handsome adolescent was still growing, still a greedy eater, but his gastric system seemed stabilized. As I write now, he's four years old. "Svelte" has expanded to solid, bordering on hefty — a muscular armful to lift.

The peach tints on his white coat, faintly visible, are still distinctive. Our vet once called him a "flame point" cat. Research, however, convinced me this is an error. The Cat Fanciers' Association describes "flame point" or "red point" cats as a type of "colorpoint shorthair." The latter, explains the CFA, are "pointed cats of Siamese ancestry and colors in other than the four traditional Siamese colors — seal, chocolate, blue and lilac point." *But* the colored "points" on these cream-bodied cats always include legs and face mask. Alex's markings are confined to his ears and tail, with an added hint of color along his back. His pointy triangular face and bright blue eyes (unlike most white cats, their color never changed) do hint at some Siamese ancestry — yet this must be pretty distant or diluted.

Alex's other physical anomaly is his falsetto voice. Instead of "niouw" and other conventional feline vocalizations, he emits high-pitched squeals. Even his purr sounds *castrato.* Not very macho or mellifluous. But he has an adventurous live-wire personality. He's athletic and playful — also skittish and jumpy. A bit fearful (or anti-social?), he vanishes from view the moment a stranger enters the house. He and Molly are sort of buddies. Indoors she rejects his romping overtures, but they scamper and chase each other around the yard the way Freddy and his sisters used to. Miraculously, Alex has roused Angela out of her customary lethargy to shadow-box briefly at mealtimes now and then — as Freddy and Felicia used to mock-wrestle while awaiting their dinner.

Toward me, he's sporadically affectionate. So far, he's too hyperactive to relax on a lap. Spends many nights nestled by me in bed and greets me with effusive nuzzles when I get up. Headstrong and self-indulgent, bright but not cooperative, Alex has been quick to learn but slow to adopt proper manners. He well *knows,* for instance, that he mustn't dive into his sisters' food dishes — yet I still need to monitor his obedience at each meal.

Let's hope my exuberant little man will mellow with time to become a substantial asset to our household. Together with gentle, lazy Angela and demure, winsome Molly, he fills out my Fourth Generation with panache. No member of this trio can compare with Toby for near-perfection in a pet — or with Lucy and Freddy for my deepest attachment. But they all enrich my life and I wouldn't part with a single one.

· 24 ·

A Vital Afterthought
Providing for Survivors

Wen we speak of parting with pets, we usually mean *they* leave *us*. Some may move to another home, as Supan, Casey, Tim, Cindy, Chico, Travis and Queen all did, for diverse reasons, when they left me. More often they die, as did ten of the cats I've told you about — plus an eleventh, Charlie, presumed to have died.

But of course it also happens that *we* are the ones to leave *them*.

I don't mean owners who deliberately relinquish pets they care little about. That's a whole separate issue of commitment — tremendously important in humane affairs but outside the scope of this book. Here, we're talking only about owners who cherish dogs and cats they'd like to keep for life. At times these animal lovers find themselves obliged, not by their own choice, to separate from their pets.

Some are forced by relocation: the family is moving somewhere their animals can't accompany them. This might be limited-choice new housing with a strict "no pets" policy; or a job in a primitive or hazardous area; or assignment to a military base; or a move to a jurisdiction with punitive quarantine restrictions on incoming animals. One British couple I knew who worked in Canada for many years left their dogs with Canadian friends when they returned back home to retire. Otherwise, on arrival in Britain, the pets would have been confined for six months before being released to live with them. Since then, the country's draconian laws to keep the U.K. free of rabies have been partly relaxed.

Yet by far the most common reason we leave the pets we love is — no surprise! — our incapacitation or death. We depart on a one-way trip to the nursing home or cemetery. Our animals remain behind. What happens to them then?

The best-case scenario involves no disruptive change in the pets' lives. Family members or good friends, who already know and get along well with the animals, immediately take full responsibility for their care and well-being. The pets will of course miss their departed owner. They'll need to adapt to new people and different household routines — but they'll adjust. Ideally, too, their new arrangements have been confirmed, with the original owner's knowledge and approval, *before* he or she has to bid them a final goodbye.

At the other extreme is a horror scenario. For some inexcusable reason, *no* provision has been made for the deceased person's pets. Nobody wants them or knows anyone willing to take them. The animals could die of neglect in their empty home. They could be abandoned at large to starve. Or they might be turned in to animal control, to be put down at the public shelter unless quickly adopted. Unfortunately, most orphaned pets surrendered to shelters are considered too old to appeal to adopters. (And that includes pedigreed dogs of many popular breeds.) Add the traumatic effect on their temperament and behavior from being rudely torn out of a secure, familiar home and dumped in a lonely cage at a strange institution. Small wonder many are stressed enough to be judged "unadoptable" — and soon euthanized.

Now and then, with extraordinary luck, disaster is averted.

My late friend Carolyn, for example, lived with a slender black cat. She hadn't made advance provisions in case she predeceased her pet — but that was understandable. Barton was a very old cat, maybe 17 or 18. And Carolyn was a vigorous woman in her early 60's with a busy advertising career and a full extracurricular life of sport, social and cultural activities. But then she was stricken suddenly and fatally by a one-two punch: cancer plus massive stroke. She had no immediate family survivors; she had made no will; she had designated no caretaker. The elderly Barton was abruptly left alone in a deserted house.

At first, a neighbor stopped by daily to feed her (Barton was a she). But what was to become of this aged animal — afflicted with a pesky skin ailment, to boot — who had been attached to just one person in one home for so many years? Carolyn's close friends Elinor and Bob, who were helping to organize some of her affairs, couldn't bear the thought of having Barton put to sleep by a vet. Nor did they dare take her in themselves, knowing that their own longtime "only" cat wouldn't tolerate this. So they got on the phone to every cat fancier they knew.

Small miracle! A couple who had recently lost their own geriatric cat agreed to adopt Barton. Not only did they give her a cozy, serene home. Sparing no effort or expense, they took her to a veterinary specialist who successfully treated her skin problem. During the year or so she lived with them, Barton developed an ardent crush on the husband. She spent hours cuddled on his lap or snuggled in his bed. Then — a contented, cosseted pet — she died peacefully in the bosom of her new family.

Moral of the story? Once in a great while a happy ending *can* befall a pet forsaken without any warning, safeguards or prospects. But let's not forget that Barton was spared a miserable end *only* because Carolyn was lucky enough to have friends like Elinor and Bob. Can any of us afford to be as irresponsible as she — gambling survival of our beloved pets on an exceptional last-minute rescue by some dedicated benefactor?

No one, you'll agree, should knowingly run that risk. *Everyone* should plan for unforeseen emergency. Even the youngest and healthiest pet keepers are vulnerable to a freak accident or devastating illness, leaving their animals forsaken. Anyone, any day, can be hit by the proverbial truck — or struck down by a sudden unpredictable ailment. The 34-year-old daughter of one of my friends died from a brain aneurysm. Her grieving mother, living hundreds of miles away, then had to make room for the three bereft grandcats she inherited. For seniors, who face a shorter future and rely more than most on their animals' companionship, the need to make posthumous arrangements for the pets is imperative.

Which brings me to my own situation.

As I finish this book, the two middle-aged female cats and

one youngish male I've just written about share my home. All of us are in reasonably good health. My own age makes me unarguably "old" but I'm still relatively active despite a debilitating lung disease. (You'll recall from a previous chapter that an early diagnosis of emphysema over three decades ago impelled me to quit smoking — which in turn led to a change of heart about readmitting cats into my home life.) How much longer will each of our family members survive? Which pets, present or future, will be here with me the day I depart? Anyone's guess. But I know I don't want *any* pet to outlive me without providing, before I go, for its safe landing and attentive care.

Like Carolyn –– who surely never imagined her cat would outlive her — I've been pretty much of a loner throughout life. By choice, I remained single. There were enjoyable affairs and a couple of marriage proposals I gave serious thought to — but the one man I'd gladly have wed on the spot never asked me. My pets have been my children. Again like Carolyn, I was an only child. (My obituary, too, will read "no immediate survivors.") Yet I'm more family-oriented than she was, on warm terms with several relatives I keep in touch with. And *un*like Carolyn, for many years I've had a properly executed will, with a trusted executor named to be in charge of my estate.

Just recently, however, I revised my will expressly for the benefit of my pets.

All the earlier versions had contained specific instructions *for my estate executor* about any surviving cats for whom I couldn't find suitable new homes before my death. Thus my pets weren't *un*provided for.

Yet I wasn't wholly satisfied with this assignment. I don't want to burden the cousin I've appointed as executor with the chore of resettling my pets. It's true that she — along with two

other cousins named as alternates, in case she's unavailable —
happen to be animal lovers (as well as lawyers). I know that any
of these relatives would seek to fulfill my wishes scrupulously and
compassionately. *But* not one of the three lives in my state. Each
knows my community only as an occasional visitor; all have family responsibilities closer to their own homes. The normal duties
of estate administration will keep my executor quite busy enough,
managing the disposition of my assets and household affairs from
afar, *without* also having to worry about the fate of my surviving
animals.

This whole issue is, in fact, quite complex. I summarized it at
the end of my earlier book, *The Pet Surplus: What Every Dog and
Cat Owner Can Do to Help Reduce It* (Xlibris, 2001). A book by
David Congalton and Charlotte Alexander, *When Your Pet Out-
lives You* (NewSage Press, 2002), explores the subject in detail.
The Humane Society of the United States offers a free kit, *Providing for Your Pet's Future Without You*, which can be obtained
by phoning 202-452-1100 or emailing *petsinwills@hsus.org*.
Among several informative websites devoted to the topic is *www.
estateplanningforpets.org*.

Here, I'll just briefly cover some key points related to my own
end-of-life circumstances and personal preferences.

First priority is *immediate/transitional care* for the pets. No
matter how informal, these measures are vital. Emergency arrangements should take effect from the first *day* I'm unable to
attend to the cats myself. I appoint a caregiver (with an alternate
specified, in case the first person is unavailable when the time
comes) who agrees to take full *temporary* responsibility for my
animals. This could be a matter of days — or weeks. It could last
longer if, for example, I spend terminal time in a hospital or nursing home, or if it takes several months to probate my will.

My pets' temporary caregiver needn't be a close friend or relative. But she must be someone I trust unreservedly with their well-being. In this interim period she'll be free to house my cats at her discretion. She may decide to keep them in her own home, or in a foster home, or at a boarding facility she approves of. She'll have my confidence to act *in my pets' best interests* — choosing the same solutions I myself would favor. Her expenses on behalf of my animals will be covered by my estate. Her responsibilities and contact information will be made known to my lawyer, doctor, family, friends, near neighbors — anyone who could be helpful or useful.

The big challenge is the *long* term. Who will be responsible for the ultimate fate of the cat companions who survive me? Until recently, as I mentioned, my estate executor was entrusted with finding them *permanent* new homes — preferably but not necessarily together — within a reasonable time period stipulated in my will. (What will happen to any animals not successfully re-homed at the end of that time? I'll come to that later.)

But if this is no longer to be a task for my executor, what other options exist? None of those cited in most current humane publications fully satisfies me:

• **A care-for-life institution.** So-called "retirement homes" or "sanctuaries" guarantee lifelong housing for orphaned pets in a group facility. Many are annexes added to long-established animal shelters. Standards of comfort, care and individual attention to the animals from staff and volunteers vary widely. So do the fees, which generally are high. Some institutions will try to place the pet(s) in a new family home if the bequeathing owner requests. But this is hard to do because most bequeathed animals are far from young.

- **A veterinary school pet center** is a variant on the above. Among the colleges of veterinary medicine offering long-term care programs for bereaved companion animals are those at Kansas State University, Purdue University, Oklahoma State University and Texas A&M University. Obviously, *any* lifecare institution needs to be exhaustively investigated and inspected before one's pets are committed to its custody.

But my problem with all such facilities has nothing to do with the rating of their services or costs. Rather, I'm opposed to the basic principle: uproot animals accustomed to a shared life as family companions and consign them to lonely subsistence as institutional inmates. Yes, they survive physically. But all *quality* in their lives — the zest and spirit and affection enjoyed by a secure member of a loving household — would be extinguished. (Dogs appear even more demoralized than cats.) Though innocent of any crime, they'd be warehoused like prisoners serving a life sentence without parole. For my own pets, I emphatically reject this fate worse than death.

- **Special adoption placement by a humane society.** The San Francisco SPCA is one of the animal shelters offering a customized service to place bereaved pets in new homes. Their Sido Program is named for an 11-year-old sheltie mix whose owner had stipulated should be put to sleep after her own death. But the shelter saved Sido, and the little dog lived another five good years with a new family. The society's members and other contributors can register in this special adoption program for any pets that may outlive them. There are donation fees but no residency requirements. As stated in its literature, the San Francisco SPCA "provides exceptional care and attention in placing these pets in loving new homes… The pledge of the Sido Program to its members — to take in and re-home their cats and dogs — is one that we honor and take great pride in fulfilling."

Similar programs are available at a half-dozen or more other prominent shelters around the country. However, *any* pet owner who is an active member and donor to his local humane society can always try to arrange in advance with that organization to take custody of his surviving animals and make an extra-special effort to re-home them successfully.

I wholeheartedly approve of such arrangements! I wouldn't hesitate to avail myself *if* all my private initiatives failed *and* a shelter I know well and admire agreed to cooperate.

• **A pet trust.** Recommended by many humane experts, this option is increasingly popular and accessible. Pet trusts are authorized by law in a growing number of states, my own among them, and Federal legislation has been introduced. Because a financial bequest cannot be left directly *to* an animal (which is classified as "property" under the law), money is left instead to a human beneficiary to be used *in trust* for the animal. The most reliable and widely endorsed type is the "inter vivos" (between the living) trust, immediately enforceable. This takes effect upon signing, while the owner is still alive, and safeguards his animals even when he becomes ill or incapacitated before death. He can also amend or revoke its provisions while he lives.

Here, for example, is how a living trust would work for my pets: First, I'd select and reach agreement with a *permanent* caretaker for my surviving cats. Then, I'd legally appoint that person as a beneficiary (ideally naming an alternate, in case the first becomes unavailable). Separately, I'd designate someone else as trustee. The trustee manages the funds I place into the trust for the cats' support and supervises the caretaking beneficiary, to ensure that my pets' needs are being met according to my wishes. The trustee might be my attorney, or the executor of my estate, or some other responsible administrator. The terms of the trust would become operative right away, guaranteeing care of my cats in case I must first spent time in a hospital or nursing home before my death.

In principle, the pet trust strikes me as a fine idea. In practice, though, it fails to suit my own needs and priorities in *two* key respects.

First and foremost, I don't like bequeathing my surviving pets to what is, in effect, a paid adopter. While I'm happy to earmark sums for, say, my cats' exceptional veterinary expenses as they get older, I'm not at all happy with the notion of subsidizing their daily maintenance in their next home. This smacks of hired foster care, like the publicly funded programs supporting homeless children. Rather, what I envision for my pets is an unselfish welcome into a new "forever" family — one which expects no monetary compensation..

Second, even swallowing objections to subsidized adoption —– which at least has the virtue of keeping the cats together — a "living pet trust" pressures me to decide very early (prematurely!) on *one* permanent caretaker to take in all my pets at once. What if my cats prove easier to re-home if split up to live with different families? What if a more desirable or motivated candidate turns up later, while I'm still functional? I'd need to re-do the trust.

In any case, *no* suitable candidate for the job of permanent caretaker/beneficiary came to my mind. A pet trust simply wouldn't work for me. This left just one option that *did* appeal to me, very much:

- **A pet executor/guardian.** My preference, I decided, is to appoint a special representative, separate from my estate executor, to be responsible *exclusively* for my pets. This "pet executor" would serve as the cats' pro tempore guardian and execute my testamentary wishes on their behalf.

I use the word "guardian" here in its classic sense. (As a warm-and-fuzzy euphemism for "owner," it's become politically correct usage among some humane professionals.) A child's legal guardian administers the minor's affairs until the child attains a mature enough age to manage on his or her own. A pet's guardian remains in charge until the animal is settled in a permanent new home — where its next owner takes over full responsibility.

In the newly revised version of my will, my cats' guardian *won't* fill the role of permanent pet caretaker. She's free if she wishes to adopt one or more of my cats privately, but is not expected to do so. Nor will her duties continue open-ended. Within a finite period of several months, specified both in the will and an attached letter of agreement between us, she'll be responsible for placing my surviving cats — any which I couldn't succeed in placing myself before my departure — in suitable adoptive homes. While engaged in the search, she'll use her own judgment about where to house the animals, their medical care, anything related to their temporary support. She may employ whatever means she chooses — networking, advertising, humane societies, veterinary hospitals — to locate hospitable families she screens and approves of. Her expenses will be reimbursed by funds from my estate and, at the conclusion of her service, she will be paid an executor's fee.

What happens if the surviving cats can't all be successfully re-homed within the specified time period? Their guardian has discretion to extend the time if she is convinced this would greatly improve chances of a desirable adoption for one or more pets. But at the end of the search, she is instructed to have a veterinarian euthanize any animals for which suitable new homes could not be found. They will *not* be condemned to linger indefinitely in some boarding facility or group institution — the fate worse than death.

How did I select my pet executor/guardian?

Luckily, I already knew a well-qualified candidate: a freelance pet sitter whose services I've employed on several occasions. She also happens to be an excellent choice as *short-term* caretaker immediately after my death or incapacitation. So the two jobs can be combined. If she hadn't agreed to our arrangement, I know one or two other trustworthy animal caregivers in the community I wouldn't hesitate to approach.

Only one detail is lacking: designation of an *alternate* pet executor/guardian if my appointee is unable to fill the role when the time comes. In that event, responsibility for the pets reverts to the executor of my estate.

I'm convinced this arrangement is the next best thing to my *first* choice. That, I repeat, is to line up good successor homes for my feline family myself, *before* I must leave them. Wouldn't that be your first choice too?

Who knows, though, if I'll have enough time and strength and resources to organize my pets' future on my own before my exit? One thing I know for sure. As long as I'm capable of enjoying them and embracing them and being soothed and intrigued and revitalized by them, I want never to live a day without my cat companions.

Photograph Captions

Front cover: TOBY and JENNY, winter 1982-83

203. ANGELA, October 3, 2005, two weeks after adoption
212. CHARLIE, October 2, 2006, eleven days after adoption
222. ALEX, July 14, 2009
233. ALEX and MOLLY looking ahead, June 22, 2008

Back cover: The author with ANGELA, April 2011.

About the Author

SUSAN M. SEIDMAN has been writing professionally for five decades. Since 1978 she has worked independently as a freelance journalist and advertising consultant. Earlier, she was a senior editor with the Foreign Policy Association, a copywriter with American Heritage Publishing Co., and the circulation promotion manager of Réalités in America.

While her published work has included gardening, travel, international affairs, vision handicaps and social commentary, her chief interest has long been companion animals. Her articles about them have appeared in *Cat Fancy, Modern Maturity* (now *AARP The Magazine), Cats* Magazine and elsewhere. They cover how-to topics — equipping pets with reliable identification, planning for animals who outlive their owners, coping with two household pets who can't get along — as well as veterinary health and some highly controversial issues: Should we allow pet cats to circulate freely outdoors? Are "no kill" animal shelters the right or wrong approach to caring for homeless dogs and cats?

Ms. Seidman's previous book, *The Pet Surplus: What Every Dog and Cat Owner Can Do to Help Reduce It* (Xlibris, 2001) was widely praised by professionals in the animal-protection field. Among the reviews —

"If you ever wondered what you could do to help animals, this book provides a clear and concise path towards making a difference. Seidman does a remarkable job..." (American Humane Association)

"As well-researched and readable a text as you could hope to find on this subject, *Pet Surplus* is also full of surprises..." (*ASPCA Animal Watch*)

"An excellent publication for members of the general public. Chock-full of details...will be an eye-opener...." (*Animal Sheltering*, published by The Humane Society of the United States)

Ms. Seidman has done extensive volunteer work with humane societies and currently shares her Long Island home with three cats.

CPSIA information can be obtained at www.ICGtesting.com
Printed in the USA
LVOW131722200612

286970LV00013B/16/P

9 780615 480589